INTELLIGENT GUIDE TO ENTERPRISE BPM

REMOVE SILOS TO UNLEASH PROCESS POWER

INTELLIGENT GUIDE TO ENTERPRISE BPM:

REMOVE SILOS TO UNLEASH PROCESS POWER

Software AG

This book was a collaborative effort written by enterprise business process management experts: Patrick Buech, Rob Davis, Christina Heller, Joerg Klueckmann, Marie Kuppler, Heiko Passauer, Sven Roeleven, Georg Simon, Katrina Simon, Thomas Stoesser, Nina Uhl, Evelyn Uhlrich and Bruce Williams. The authors acknowledge Nancy Beckman and Jane Sarver for their guidance and assistance in the preparation of this book.

June 2012

ISBN #: 1620300877

Published by Software AG

ABOUT SOFTWARE AG

Software AG is the global leader in Business Process Excellence. Our 40 years of innovation include the invention of the first high-performance transactional database, Adabas; the first business process analysis platform, ARIS; and the first B2B server and SOA-based integration platform, webMethods.

We offer our customers end-to-end Enterprise Business Process Management (EBPM) solutions delivering low Total-Cost-of-Ownership and high ease of use. Our industry-leading brands, ARIS, webMethods, Adabas, Natural, CentraSite, Terracotta and IDS Scheer Consulting, represent a unique portfolio encompassing: process strategy, design, integration, execution and control; SOA-based integration and data management; process-driven SAP implementation; and strategic process consulting and services.

Software AG – Get There Faster.™

TABLE OF CONTENTS

CHAPTER 1

ENTERPRISE BPM—Remove Silos to Unleash Process Power

INTRODUCTION

You are about to get a lot smarter about Enterprise Business Process Management (EBPM). By reading this book, you'll learn how successful organizations are able to adapt all the time to changing market conditions. You'll see why Enterprise BPM is the key to aligning corporate strategy with operational processes and the underlying IT landscape. You'll discover best practices, and learn how to avoid pitfalls and achieve business results faster on your road to Enterprise BPM.

You'll find out the destination is well worth the journey. Because once you reach the state of Enterprise BPM, you'll have processes that work in total alignment with your business objectives. You'll be that agile enterprise, easily able to navigate changes. And your business and IT teams will work as a single unit. Departmental processes will be "out of the box" and integrated enterprise-wide. Along the way to Enterprise BPM, you'll realize measurable business results and process improvements—because process improvement is a continuous process itself!

The following chapters will detail how to reach major milestones in your Enterprise BPM journey:

- Chapter 2: Business Process Analysis: From corporate strategy to process design
- Chapter 3: Enterprise Architecture Management: From IT planning to IT landscape monitoring
- Chapter 4: Business Process Management: From process design to automation
- Chapter 5: Process Intelligence: From automation to performance measurement
- Chapter 6: Governance, Risk and Compliance Management: From documenting compliance controls to managing risks and compliance

So where should your EBPM journey begin? The answer is rather simple: start anywhere, expand everywhere.

A COMPANY'S ARCHITECTURE IN A NUTSHELL

All companies are basically built using the same architecture—no matter if they are big or small, in Europe, Asia or the Americas. All have a business model, processes and IT applications. The business model describes what products and services are produced for which markets, who the customers and business partners are, and the company's plan for the future.

Processes, however, are built for each company based on the business model. A bank, for example, has different processes than a consumer goods/retail or a chemical/pharmaceutical company. Nevertheless, all processes, no matter the industry or business, exist to support the business model. Each process exists at varying levels of maturity—from ad hoc and manual processes to well documented and automated processes. The backbone of the layer of processes is IT. Information technology makes sure the business processes have the applications and data they need to be up and running.

In most companies, business models change often. New products are launched. Acquisitions take place and must be integrated. New markets must be conquered. This, of course, directly impacts a company's processes.

Keeping up is a never-ending job. Existing processes must be modified and new processes established. Processes from an acquired organization must be aligned and integrated. Also, the IT landscape has to be adjusted. That means existing applications must be changed, new applications introduced and acquired applications integrated.

The problem lies in that this adaptation isn't very fluid in most organizations because the business model, the process layer and IT applications are not well connected. In fact, there's often a dramatic disconnect. If the strategy changes, it's hard to see which processes are affected and how to change them. If a process needs to change, it's hard to figure out which IT systems are affected and how they must be changed to support the new process. Once the process is up and running in the application layer, it's almost impossible for most of the organization to prove that processes support the new strategy. With such a disconnect between strategy, process and applications, it is hard—if not impossible—to adapt quickly to changing business models and new market conditions.

To stay agile and competitive, every business should be concerned about how fast it can adjust to business model changes and how fast its processes and its supporting application landscape can adapt.

BPM vendors are beginning to address this problem. For example, Software AG answers this concern by adding an agility layer that makes all processes explicit and manageable. The agility layer is the key to keeping a business adaptive because it directly interconnects strategy, processes and IT. It's there to help your business continuously adapt to new market conditions.

THE AGILITY LAYER

Processes are the lifelines of your business, and they can only work as an agility layer between corporate strategy and IT when you nurture them sufficiently. BPM was made exactly for this.

Unfortunately, BPM is not implemented optimally or at all in most organizations. Sure, companies may have plenty of process improvement projects, some more than they can keep track of. These projects, though, are stuck in disparate departmental silos using different tools and methodologies. They don't interact with each other very well or at all. A department may have "perfect" processes. But what's the real business value if a process isn't well connected to its predecessor and its successor—and benefits only one business unit but harms another?

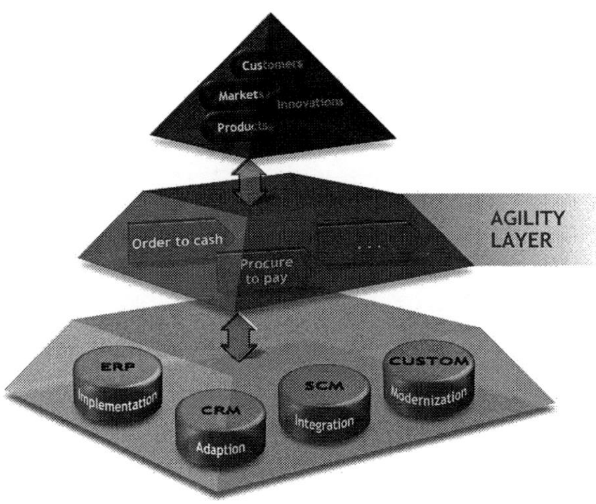

Figure 1-1: The "agility layer": Applications built to last, processes & integration built to change

That's where the agility layer comes into play [See Figure 1-1]. By making all your processes explicit and improving them with an end-to-end approach that follows your business objectives, you can unleash process power for your entire enterprise. This layer is the key to breaking up the different silos and bringing them together in a sustainable corporate-wide program, spanning all departments. The result is Enterprise BPM, a holistic end-to-end view of your process landscape that helps you to understand the impact of a new strategy on your processes and IT layer. Using an integrated BPM software suite based on industry-leading technology and best practice methodologies, you can define your corporate strategy and then model, analyze, execute and monitor processes to improve performance all the time. This suite must be enhanced by teamwork—a team that blends talent from business and IT.

You may think business doesn't understand IT and IT isn't interested in business. But quite the opposite is often true! In many organizations, business people are very much interested in the work IT is doing. Likewise, IT people would very much like to understand the business impact of their work. To be that agile enterprise, business and IT—in fact, all BPM stakeholders—must be connected through a collaborative Enterprise BPM environment with strong process governance. This is the way to unleash process power and get the maximum business value from BPM!

ENTERPRISE BPM LIFECYCLE

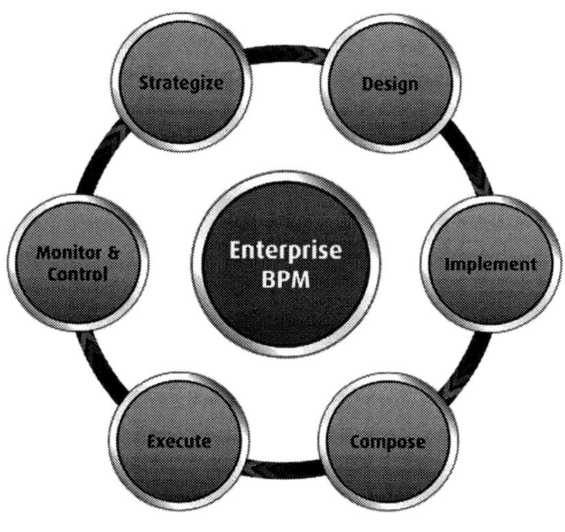

Figure 1-2: The Enterprise BPM Lifecycle

So how can you create a sustainable Enterprise BPM program in your organization? Ideally, you would:

- Start by describing your corporate strategy and then break it down to Key Performance Indicators (KPIs)
- Design your process and IT landscape and link strategy and KPIs
- Transfer business process models to technical models. Business and IT will collaborate on them supported by governance technology
- Technically enrich the processes you want to execute using IT and create a user interface
- Deploy the processes and make them operational
- Monitor and improve the executed processes, and then manage risks and possible compliance issues

If the corporate strategy changes, you'd know which processes and IT systems to adjust and how. You'd see instantly if the related KPIs were met. In the meantime, you'd also set up an Enterprise BPM competence team with both business and IT people. You'd establish collaboration between the different stakeholders to improve processes using transparent and solid process governance. Job done! You would have implemented Enterprise BPM and built that agility layer.

But since we don't live in a perfect world, it's not always possible to start at the beginning of the lifecycle and then move in order to the next step. That's the beauty of Enterprise BPM. You can start anywhere and expand everywhere. In fact, you should start in the area that is most important to your business objectives and create your own short-term goals and long-term vision. For some, risk management is most important. For others, it's visibility or automation. It's better to start small and think big than to never start at all. Enterprise BPM is the vision and the entry points are the potential places to begin.

Enterprise BPM lets you start at five different entry points:

Business Process Analysis (BPA)

Enterprise Architecture (EA) Management

Business Process Management (BPM)

Process Intelligence (PI)

Governance, Risk & Compliance (GRC) Management

No matter where you start, you'll put that agility layer in place so your business will be adaptable, agile and ready for change! But keep on thing in mind. All BPM projects, no matter if you start with BPA, EA or BPM should be integrated in one EBPM program to get a holistic picture of your enterprise and with this to groundbreaking process improvement results.

Entry Point #1: BUSINESS PROCESS ANALYSIS (BPA)

Successful implementation of the BPA entry point will mean you have successfully documented, standardized, harmonized, managed—as well as analyzed and improved—your business processes. Process improvements are aligned with optimization goals, such as cost savings, time savings and quality.

With BPA, you'll be able to:

- Understand the business environment
- Identify the strategy and key objectives
- Analyze critical success factors
- Define and follow standards
- Record an enterprise process landscape
- Define end-to-end processes
- Identify improvement opportunities
- Develop to-be concept and processes
- Transform the organization
- Implement BPM governance model

BPA Best Practices

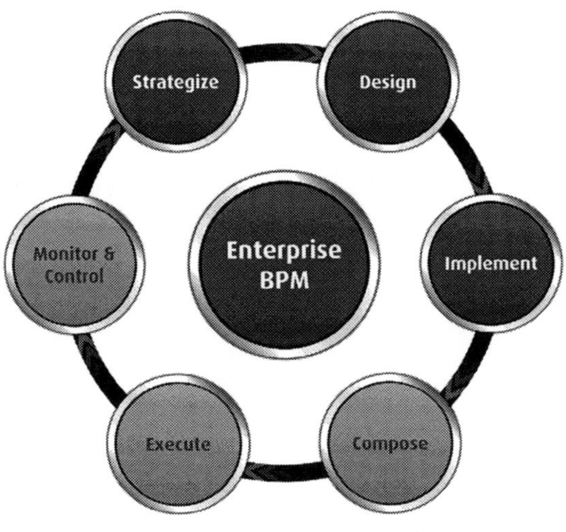

Figure 1-3: The BPA and EA entry points in the EBPM lifecycle: Strategize, Design and Implement

1. **Understand and support the corporate strategy**

If you don't know what your corporate strategy looks like, you can't design your processes to achieve it. You'll also fall short when you have to prove at a later stage how your BPA project has contributed to corporate strategy. Model your strategy with the right methodology (business segment matrix, critical success factors, SWOT analysis, balanced scorecard, cause-and-effect analysis, KPI trees) and tools that let you map your strategy with processes.

2. **Plan for change and address politics**

"If you want to make enemies, try to change something." That's what 28th U.S. President Woodrow Wilson said. There are several factors that might make it hard to reach the first milestone successfully. If you discover the as-is processes, you have created transparency. Not everyone is a big fan of transparency. Make sure that people understand that it is not your intention to reduce the workforce but to use it more effectively and efficiently. You might have to change processes from as-is to to-be. To do this, you should have some change management initiatives in place.

3. **Find allies and establish a Center of Excellence (C-Level sponsorship)**

You can't change the way your organization works alone. You need allies who support you. The best approach is to find one in each involved department. You definitely need people from business and IT. It is critical to get sponsorship from C-Level. This will help you to cope with resistance. Bring all stakeholders together in a Center of Excellence. This could be a face-to-face meeting or a virtual working group.

4. **Manage expectations and define measures**

Start with a few focus areas first to show value before tackling the entire enterprise. Set clear and achievable expectations. And don't forget to define measures for success and clear, achievable KPIs.

5. **Establish solid process governance**

Process governance manages the process of process management and the related roles and responsibilities. Not everyone should be able to model and/or change a process. Without process governance, your BPA project will be a mess.

6. **Define and follow standards**

   You need to define and follow standards to ensure consistent interpretation of your process models. If everyone uses different tools and methodologies for describing a process, you'll end up with the proverbial Tower of Babel.

7. **Never forget the Five Ws of BPA. Think carefully.**

- Why you are modeling? You must ensure the benefits of your model align with corporate objectives.
- Who are the customers for the models? An IT designer will have different expectations than a business analyst.
- What are you modeling? Is it a sales process, and where does it start and end? What products does it handle?
- When will the models be relevant? Distinguish between as-is and to-be processes and consider the lifetime of models.
- Where will the models be used? Models published on the intranet need to be visual and fully linked so that people can easily navigate them. Models that will be used for documentation need to rely more on information defined in model/object attributes.

And, there's one H. Don't forget HOW you will model your processes. Define methods, tools, architecture, standards and reference models before you start. You will also need to think about modeling notations like the Event-driven Process Chain (EPC) or Business Process Model and Notation (BPMN). The notation should follow the audience who is consuming the models. There may also be requirements to use standard process frameworks, such as ITIL and SCOR, or industry-specific reference models, such as eTOM for the telecommunications industry. Do never forget, standards are critical.

BPA Pitfalls to Avoid

No standards

A variety of process modeling tools are available. Some use Visio®, others ARIS and some describe their processes in Microsoft® PowerPoint®. Process models are stored on the local hard disk; some are on file servers. Others cannot be found. Everyone uses different objects/shapes to describe the same thing. This is indeed the worst case.

Strategy is strategy and process is process

Management knows that a corporate strategy is important. It takes several meetings to agree on it but then it stays in the board room. If you ask employees what the corporate strategy looks like, you barely get an answer. It's even harder for employees to understand how they contribute to the strategy.

Modeling only the "happy path"

It's tempting to model only the processes where everything runs smoothly. But if you do this you can't find improvement potentials.

Keeping models secret

Processes are for everyone. Don't keep them secret in your repository. Share them with your organization or even beyond. But don't forget the Five Ws.

Forgetting input and output

A process consumes input and transfers it to an output—and hopefully adds value along the way. If you design a process or a process step, make sure you also document the input and the output.

Not differentiating between model designer and consumer

The person creating a process model should always keep in mind who the consumer will be. A business person has different requirements than an IT person. The best is to have one model with different views on it.

Everyone can model everything—no governance

Process transformation needs a process of process management. You need to set up a governance structure around rights and roles. Not everyone should have the right to model or change every process. Don't underestimate the effort of developing and implementing governance. It is strongly recommended to use technology as governance support.

Entry Point #2: ENTERPRISE ARCHITECTURE (EA) MANAGEMENT

Corporate IT resources constitute a complex system. An Enterprise Architecture (EA) describes this system and establishes standards for managing and transforming it. Understanding the EA system requires a number of views: business processes, information, applications and technologies. Multiple perspectives must be taken into account, ranging from the enterprise view at a highly abstract level to detailed views of individual business units, design aspects and physical systems.

Very often, IT and business professionals are unable to align their activities because BPA and EA management initiatives are separate. As a consequence, IT is still often the famous black box with no transparency into how IT investments actually support business objectives and processes. For this reason, an Enterprise BPM program brings together BPA and EA to improve the business value of IT investments. The need to operationalize IT strategy—which itself must be aligned with the business strategy—is another reason why the integration between business and IT is a must to unleash process power.

With EA management, you can:

- Derive IT requirements directly from business processes
- Deliver faster high-quality IT solutions to meet business demands
- Communicate the value of IT investments using business justification
- Articulate how IT can drive process improvement and actively support business success
- Establish a long-term IT architecture management concept to realize the company's strategy

EA Management Best Practices

1. Determine what your EA looks like

First, compile information about the IT landscape, including hardware and software. If you have done BPA, then map your IT to your process requirements using the same repository. It is critical that your documentation is accurate and up-to-date.

2. Establish IT governance

Define, establish and document the IT governance processes required within your EA management initiative. You should be able to answer:

- Who has data sovereignty?
- Who requests systems and who connects them?
- Who has access rights to what type of data?
- How does process management function with IT?
- Who is involved in the system lifecycle?

3. Roll it out

Next, roll out EA management software, including the governance processes and measures. The IT architects and architecture managers determine and verify to what extent the system descriptions are satisfied.

4. Make it public

EA management requires a broad user group, so all the concerned groups should cooperate. So it's important to do some internal marketing and persuade users that working within the EA management initiative is a worthwhile effort. Make the initiative's objectives known!

EA Management Pitfalls to Avoid

EA management is not a cure-all!

One of the most common mistakes is attempting to solve all of an organization's problems at the same time. Defining the objective properly is crucial to setting up a successful EA management system. The right plan can deliver short- and medium-term results without compromising the long-term strategy and future evolution of the business.

EA management project teams – paper tigers?

Lack of awareness of the enterprise-wide value of EA management by divisions and departments often prevents the establishment of proper organizational structures to support EA management. Rather than regarding EA management as just another trend, management needs to be convinced of the need to set up this kind of management system and equip it with the corresponding authority.

Taking a random approach to EA management processes

The implementation of EA management is often hampered by the absence of a clear, standardized definition of the EA management processes.

- How should EA management work?
- Which roles are involved?
- Where are the boundaries between different areas of responsibility?
- Which activities must be performed, in what order and by whom?

You will need a coherent, standardized method that enables smart integration of the deployed methods and tools.

EA management description—lost in translation

In many projects, the lack of a shared, enterprise-wide description method and poor integration of the different EA perspectives make it impossible to gain a holistic view of the processes and successfully implement EA management. EAs need to be incorporated into an architecture framework to avoid these problems. Such a framework must contain all the views required for an integrated architecture and provide a best practice model. Don't overlook widely accepted architecture standards, such as TOGAF, DoDAF, Zachman, IAF and ArchiMate.

Too many tools spoil the EA

Organizations often deploy a range of different tools—some developed in-house—to document business processes, manage IT systems, standardize technologies and produce blueprints of their IT environment. With such a diverse range of tools and data records, EA management is doomed to fail. Only a central repository that is fully integrated into corporate BPA initiatives, a common role-based way of capturing data and a consistent method across all views can assure EA management success.

Entry Point #3: BUSINESS PROCESS MANAGEMENT (BPM)

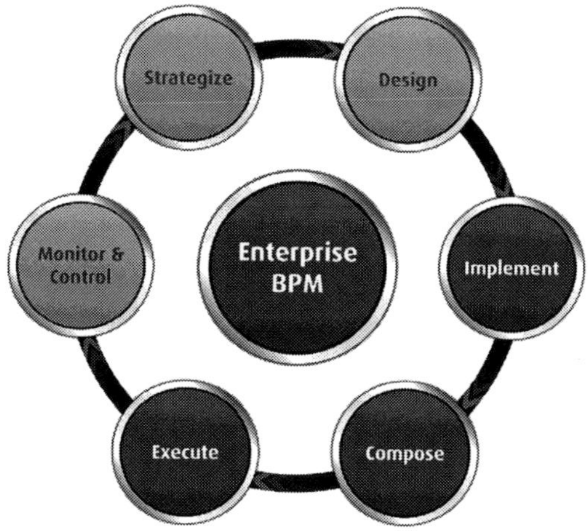

Figure 1-4: The BPM entry point in the EBPM lifecycle: Implement, Compose and Execute

It's important to build your BPM on a proven Business Process Management Suite (BPMS), such as webMethods BPMS, and to use an integration platform, such as webMethods Integration Server, to integrate with all needed IT systems that you've identified in your EA management initiative. The processes from your BPA initiative should be the blueprint/requirement for their technical execution. This way, IT can rapidly develop new process-centric applications by re-using services and increase productivity via a flexible and intuitive workflow.

With BPM, you'll be able to:

- Implement a Service-Oriented Architecture (SOA) to re-use existing IT assets
- Align your IT assets with your business processes
- Build a solid and consistent data foundation
- Implement and refine process models and business logic
- Manage and govern all your IT assets
- Provide user interfaces for process participants
- Execute business processes
- Create rules and alerts based on process KPIs
- Monitor business processes end-to-end

BPM Best Practices

1. Automate the right process

Regardless of whether you have completed BPA or not, many companies struggle to identify the right process to automate.

Here are five simple questions to ask that can provide a pragmatic way of determining whether your processes have automation potential.

- Is the process in question very "paper heavy?" Is there a paper form that gets routed to different process participants as part of the process?
- Do your process workers waste time looking for data, forms or documents that they need to complete a specific step?
- Does the process require manual duplication of data where maybe an email address has to be manually copied from one system to another?
- Do your processes "hang" because one of the process workers didn't receive an email that tells them to proceed with the next step?
- Are there any other "routine" tasks that are very time consuming or that can halt the process in its tracks if the task owner goes on holiday or simply forgets to do it one day?

If you can answer "yes" to one or more of the above, you are looking at a process with automation potential. If you are not 100% sure whether a process is a good fit for automation, or of you want to figure out what the impact of such a "yes" is, you should speak to the people who perform the process day in and day out.

2. Fulfill the right requirements: Model-to-Execute

Often, the IT department gets business requirements in a Word document, a spreadsheet, via a chat in the coffee room or even a process model. Usually, this is when the interpretation on the IT side begins. Months later, IT proudly presents the results of its hard work. The business may not be happy because it didn't get the desired results or the requirements have changed during development. Finger-pointing starts and the result is frustration on both sides.

So what's the best practice to use here? Business should create a process model that shows how it expects the process to run when implemented. Business and IT then go through the model together to get a common understanding. Business shares the model with IT and the technical folks start working on the model. If IT changes the process in a way that affects business or vice versa, a governance process starts that lets both sides work collaboratively on the model to review and approve/reject changes. This way, the models and the stakeholders are always in sync.

3. **Build a bridge from the abstract process to the work environment**

Often IT talks to business the way it would talk to an IT peer. For business, this conversation can be hard to follow, which can lead to misunderstandings and frustration. Instead, it's better to make the result of the development project more tangible by using a series of screen designs that illustrates the process flow.

4. **Get more out of existing IT assets**

Re-use existing IT assets/services to accelerate the development of new applications. Quick wins are always preferred. It helps to have a Service-Oriented Architecture (SOA) as well as SOA governance in place to know your services and to ensure proper re-use. Don't forget to sync up processes with services.

BPM Pitfalls to Avoid

Automating failures

If a process has errors, you might not solve them by just automating the process. Make sure you fix the process before you automate it.

Changing processes without involving business

Sometimes a process that comes from the business needs to be modified technically. If the modification is a technical detail, you can move on to implementing the process. But if you change the business logic, you'd better inform your business stakeholder. Work collaboratively on the process change and reach a common understanding. Collaboration and governance technology can support here.

Not having transparency about the stakeholder

It's important to know your stakeholders. They will decide at the end of the automation initiative if it was successful or not. This is why you should be in contact with them regularly.

Forgetting measurements

It is always important to prove business value. The best way to do this is with solid facts. For this, you need measurements. Make sure you know the KPIs before the automation and, of course, after you have implemented the process. Share the KPIs in your organization. Creating dashboards or mashups of information using graphical screens can help.

Believing the business doesn't care and doesn't understand

More and more "digital natives" are challenging IT. They understand what works and how long it should take to get it done. They are more than happy to tag team with IT to make their own lives easier. Often, they are very proud when the automation is done and the new application is up and running. These folks are ITs best allies.

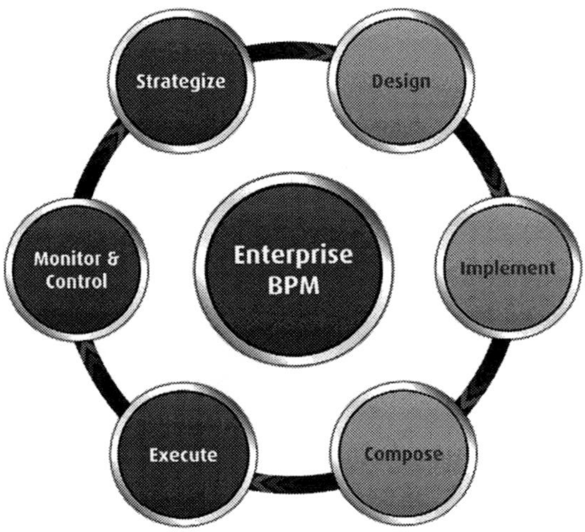

Figure 1-5: The PI and GRC entry points in the EBPM lifecycle: Execute, Monitor & Control and Strategize

Entry Point #4: PROCESS INTELLIGENCE (PI)

To measure performance, organizations typically use figures, such as revenues, profits and cash flow, which are the result of the business processes executed. However, collecting KPIs on a pure data-driven basis without linking them to the operational processes is of little benefit if the figures fail to match the defined objectives. After all, it's hard to fix things without knowing the cause of the problem.

In the Process Intelligence (PI) entry point, you'll establish process control at the strategic, tactical and operational levels. If KPIs (such as time, cost, quality or risk) deviate from the strategic objectives, the causes can be analyzed within the operational processes. Corrective action can then be taken in real-time before customers are impacted.

With PI, you'll be able to:

- Make your operational business processes transparent (automated process discovery)
- React on unforeseen events in real-time
- Define alerts, thresholds and calls-to-actions
- Measure and analyze performance in real-time
- Analyze and understand process patterns
- Recognize and manage improvements
- Identify and roll out best practice processes
- Create and share mashup dashboards with role-based KPIs
- Provide management with feedback on strategy

PI Best Practices

1. Synchronize with strategy

A process or agility layer acts as the glue between strategy and IT. Measuring how you reached corporate objectives proves your success. If one objective of the strategy was to improve sales efficiency, then gather and analyze a set of KPIs to see if the efficiency was really improved (such as order-to-cash cycle time). If you can present these results, management will see—and treasure—that the strategy was implemented.

2. Know what to measure

When it comes to PI, people usually think that the most difficult part is the technical challenge of monitoring and analyzing operational processes. Of course, this can be very challenging. The bigger challenge, however, is gaining agreement on WHAT to measure. If you measure the wrong things, you will fix the wrong problems, and you might even create new problems. For example, if you concentrate on lowering process costs, you might harm your service quality, which will lead to lower customer satisfaction, which might decrease your revenue. You get the idea. This is why you need to have a clear understanding of what you want to improve.

3. Get agreements and signatures on KPIs

Once you know how to refine your KPIs, you will need to get agreement on what you will measure. The key to this step is to make sure that the people who are responsible for the achievement of the KPI are in the room when you set up your KPI landscape. You need to be sure that everyone agrees on the limits of a KPI: when is it successful and when is it not? And the agreement should be defined on paper, and in the presence of the senior manager.

This step in defining KPIs just might help you ensure improvements to your KPIs. For example, if the owners of the KPI you are measuring haven't agreed to what you are measuring, then they might decide to change the calculations down the road to show improvements without actually achieving any. Or you might find yourself having to justify what you are measuring to your team if it didn't buy into the KPIs up front.

4. Keep things as simple as possible—but not simpler (remember the 5 Ws from the BPA best practices)

There are many processes and KPIs to measure in today's organizations. Sometimes people go crazy when they realize the power of measuring operational processes. Be warned: Don't try to measure all KPIs or just your favorite KPIs, or the ones which are the easiest to measure, or the ones which were traditionally measured. Instead, limit your KPIs to those that will provide insight into the processes you want to improve. The purpose of PI is to improve business performance. Find out which KPIs are essential for your business and which processes impact these KPIs. Measure these processes by picking the most important KPIs of the process. Also, the 5 Ws can help here. Have a look in the BPA section if you can't remember what they are all about.

PI Pitfalls to Avoid

Garbage in, garbage out

All the PI in the world won't give you a good answer if you're processing bad data. Bad data leads to bad intelligence. Be careful that you ensure the quality of data on which you base your intelligence. You'll encounter special challenges when you have to combine data from different sources. Fortunately, there are many tools and techniques available for detecting bad data and taking action.

"We already have this"

People have been creating reports and dashboards and implementing database query and business intelligence tools for years. You may find that people will look beyond the new and unique capabilities of PI and say: "We already have this." No, they don't. They may have bits and pieces, but they lack the process view that you'll get with an agility layer. If a report shows that an objective failed, you need a link to the responsible processes. Otherwise, you have no idea how to fix the problem.

PI is a secret weapon

In a PI project, you measure KPIs to see how your operational processes are performing. To avoid conflicts based on the new level of transparency, you should involve all of the key stakeholders early. Without the support of the business managers, it will be difficult to understand the business process and to find the right KPIs. You need the IT organization to support you to set up your PI software and to extract the KPIs from the different systems. Most importantly, both sides should see your PI project as their PI project. They should look forward to using the tools to improve performance and to using the project to position their requirements in the organization.

Entry Point #5: GOVERNANCE, RISK & COMPLIANCE (GRC)

Another entry point to Enterprise BPM is concerned with managing risks in your company and possible compliance issues. GRC combines BPA, EA, BPM and PI with audit-proof workflows, turning risk and compliance management into an integrated management solution—all aligned to your company's business strategy and the related processes.

With GRC, you'll be able to:

- Implement a flexible enterprise-wide compliance and risk management system
- Integrate all regulatory demands and operational risks into a single approach and Internal Control System (ICS)
- Cut costs and increase efficiencies using a workflow approach
- Prove compliance easily—you can produce relevant documentation in one click
- Update management with an up-to-the-minute dashboard
- Improve investor relations and your corporate image

GRC Best Practices

1. Use a standard risk framework as a best practice model

Stick to a framework. As your ultimate goal is to manage your risk, these risk frameworks are a best practices and principles you can apply easily within your organization.

2. Turn risks into results

When you think about your company's strategy development and execution, it's important to see risk not only as a way to protect your business but as a way to increase your business performance. Companies that succeed in turning risk into results will create competitive advantage through more efficient deployment of scarce resources, better decision-making and reduced exposure to negative events.

3. Establish a common language for risk, control and performance

Without a standard naming convention or common methodology for determining or classifying risks, compliance and business performance, assurance professionals from different disciplines are unable to share information. Risk assessments are performed multiple times by multiple assurance groups on the same risks. The processes where the risks occur are audited several times for different regulations and are probably also measured multiple times. The benefits of utilizing a common language and methodology are far reaching and include:

- Improved reporting throughout the organization
- Consistent coverage – all risks are considered
- Improved business performance – risks explain performance gaps

- Better decision making – decisions are risk based
- Less external oversight and audits – controls are standardized

4. **Enabling an integrated methodology**

For effective GRC convergence of topics such as compliance, process performance and process management, all GRC information should be available in one single solution and accessible to all appropriate parties.

GRC assurance experts, business managers and even some stakeholders will require access to regularly read, update and report on status. By eliminating information silos and redundant data entry, and taking a unique holistic approach to regulatory challenges, GRC technology provides greater efficiency, improves collaboration, and reduces the time and resource costs associated with GRC processes. GRC technology enables organizations to break down the walls between audit, risk and compliance groups and provides expanded value as organizations deploy the software across the enterprise.

GRC Pitfalls to Avoid

GRC is not separated from the business

Governance (G), Risk (R) and Compliance (C) is an integral part of the business and cannot be operated separately. GRC is actually a best practice itself. Don't wait for the law to implement these best practices, such as Sarbanes Oxley (SOX) for example. Your company needs to have good governance as well as good risk management and controls in place. This will ultimately help your organization. Implement GRC across the entire organization. Avoid a siloed approach in each discipline.

Implementing GRC distinctly from IT GRC

IT is not a backroom function. IT is a strategic function and a business enabler. You cannot separate GRC from IT GRC and get to the IT part later. Get to the IT piece of it now! IT GRC is an integral part of how you do your business. Look for synergies between GRC and IT.

Working in silos

Driven by internal reporting structures, direction from senior executives, and traditional functional roles; internal audit, risk management, and compliance professionals often are found to work in rigid silos focused on a set of departmental objectives. Information is not transparent or exchanged and accountability is not established among risk, compliance and performance groups. Each group develops their own standards, methodologies, and bodies of knowledge and best practices with their own sources. The obvious problem with overlap is inefficiency. A variety of GRC groups often assess the same issues, wasting GRC resources and management time.

To overcome the internal silo issue, a best practice is to implement an internal GRC competency center. The GRC competency center will create role clarity, eliminate redundant tasks, and enhance collaboration between the GRC leadership team and process owners.

Reliance on audits and inspections

Most organizations rely extensively on GRC experts from audit, risk management, compliance or IT to assess and report on risk and control across the enterprise. Generally speaking, regulators and professional standard setters place less reliance on management self-assessment in these areas on the basis that it lacks independence and objectivity. Such thinking has robbed management of accountability and created the silo-based approaches that exist today. It is not possible to achieve GRC convergence through audit and inspection alone.

CONCLUSION

With Enterprise BPM, you'll have an agility layer that makes it easy to transfer your corporate strategy to your operational processes and to the underlying IT applications. You can implement new business models in days, not months or years. Your organization will be more agile than ever before. But be aware—as time moves forward, things change. A process that's perfect today won't be perfect tomorrow. Markets, laws and regulations, technology, customer demands, competition, innovations and resources may degrade performance or effectiveness. Enterprise BPM is your view into these changes. It's how you'll always stay aware and adaptive.

Once you have the vision for Enterprise BPM, you'll want to choose a vendor with the software and services to help with every entry point. For example, learn about Software AG's approach at www.softwareag.com/ebpm.

Now let's take a deep dive into each possible entry point to Enterprise BPM.

CHAPTER 2

BUSINESS PROCESS ANALYSIS—Transforming Your Business by Transforming Your Processes

INTRODUCTION

Business Process Analysis (BPA) is the entry point focused on the alignment of business strategy, process design and the IT implementation of both. Effective BPA means you will have successfully documented, standardized, harmonized, managed—as well as analyzed and improved—your business processes.

BPA is one major way to reach your goals with Enterprise BPM. So let's continue your journey.

WHY BPA?

Few organizations are performing at their highest potential, so there is always room to improve processes or establish new ones. Even if you're able to implement high-quality processes now, the world doesn't stand still. So you need BPA to:

- Ensure processes continue to deliver business objectives
- Respond to the changing market and business environment
- Rapidly deliver new products and services
- Adapt to organizational change
- Ensure effective use of resources
- Take advantage of new technology
- Manage and support the complete SAP implementation lifecycle
- Establish business processes for a seamless process automation

BPA is not just about process improvement projects. It's about "transforming" your processes to deliver business objectives by re-using and optimizing your business infrastructure, which incorporates IT, people, equipment and resources. Processes are vital to all organizations, so you need to treat them as business assets to be managed and controlled. But processes are more than just an asset. "Processes are the business" so managing your business is the same as managing your processes.

"Managing the Business by Managing the Processes"

BPA is a continuous process itself. It requires the right method, approach, tools and governance. When you combine the management of processes with the management of IT, you can achieve Enterprise BPM which is the key to aligning corporate strategy with operational processes and the underlying IT landscape.

BPM isn't easy. It requires new skills and tools to be acquired and successfully deployed. It also requires difficult business issues to be tackled as well as a change to a process-centric approach to management and performance measurement. BPM is a journey and, as with all journeys, you need to know where you are going and have a roadmap for getting there. Along the way, it will be hard work. But there will be lots of benefits. You'll realize measurable process improvements, and you will find the destination is well worth the journey.

HOW TO TRANSFORM YOUR PROCESSES

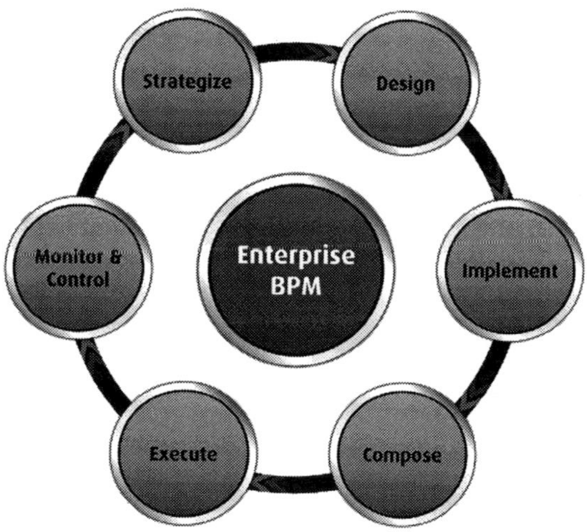

Figure 2-1: The stages of Enterprise BPM

To successfully transform your processes, you need the right tools and methods. For example, Software AG's Enterprise BPM lifecycle defines the stages you need to work through, and our ARIS and webMethods technologies provide all the tools you need.

The Enterprise BPM Lifecycle

The six phases of the Enterprise BPM lifecycle [Figure 2-1] take you through all the necessary steps to design, implement, automate and control your processes.

1. Strategize – describe corporate strategy and map it to the business processes
2. Design – define the enterprise processes, the resources that implement them and the business environment in which they operate
3. Implement – transform business models into automated processes
4. Compose – architect new processes and applications across the existing IT infrastructure
5. Execute – deploy and manage processes across systems and people
6. Monitor and Control – measure processes and real-time KPIs, analyze past history and resolve problems

BPA Roles

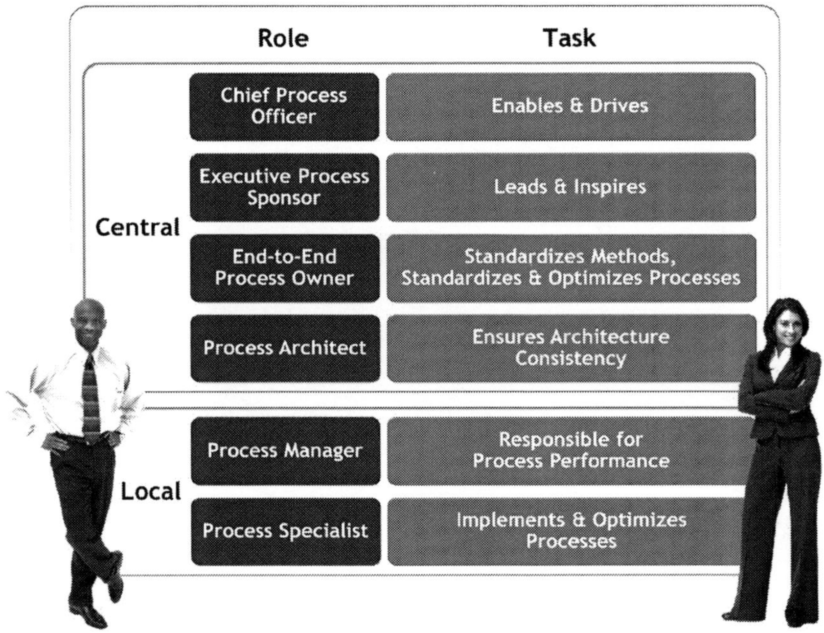

BPA Roles

Many people need to be involved in transforming processes and achieving process excellence. Some of the most important roles include:

- Chief Process Officer (CPO) – Defines process strategy and objectives; establishes a process governance structure with process owners; owns the enterprise process map; ensures core processes deliver customer-driven performance and meet strategic objectives.

- Executive Process Sponsor – Leads and inspires development of core processes to deliver the very best for customers; defines the end-to-end process vision; assigns process ownership roles and communicates ownership and accountability; and champions process developments using process as a driver of business performance.
- E2E Process Owner – Defines detailed End-to-End (E2E) process measures (KPIs); ensures the design of the E2E process; integrates and re-uses business unit processes; ensures customer satisfaction is measured and delivered and that revenue and efficiency targets are met; ensures the E2E process aligns with corporate strategy; initiates and manages E2E process improvement initiatives; promotes standardization and optimization; and agrees on IT system changes that have an impact on the process.
- Process Architect – Defines the corporate process architecture; manages the enterprise process map and secures consensus and agreement; works with end-to-end process owners and process managers to ensure architectural conformance; and works with IT to promote business service re-use.
- Process Manager – Manages day-to-day operation of business unit processes to targets set by end-to-end process owners; responsible for design of business unit processes, manages allocation of resources and ensures collection of agreed-upon KPIs; provides process infrastructure (such as documentation, systems and equipment) to support process users; and coordinates business unit process improvement.
- Process Specialist – Undertakes detailed process design, analysis and improvement using agreed-upon process standards, methods and tools; ensures processes meet process objectives and customer experience targets and are compliant with architectural standards; and verifies and validates that the process is fit-for-purpose.

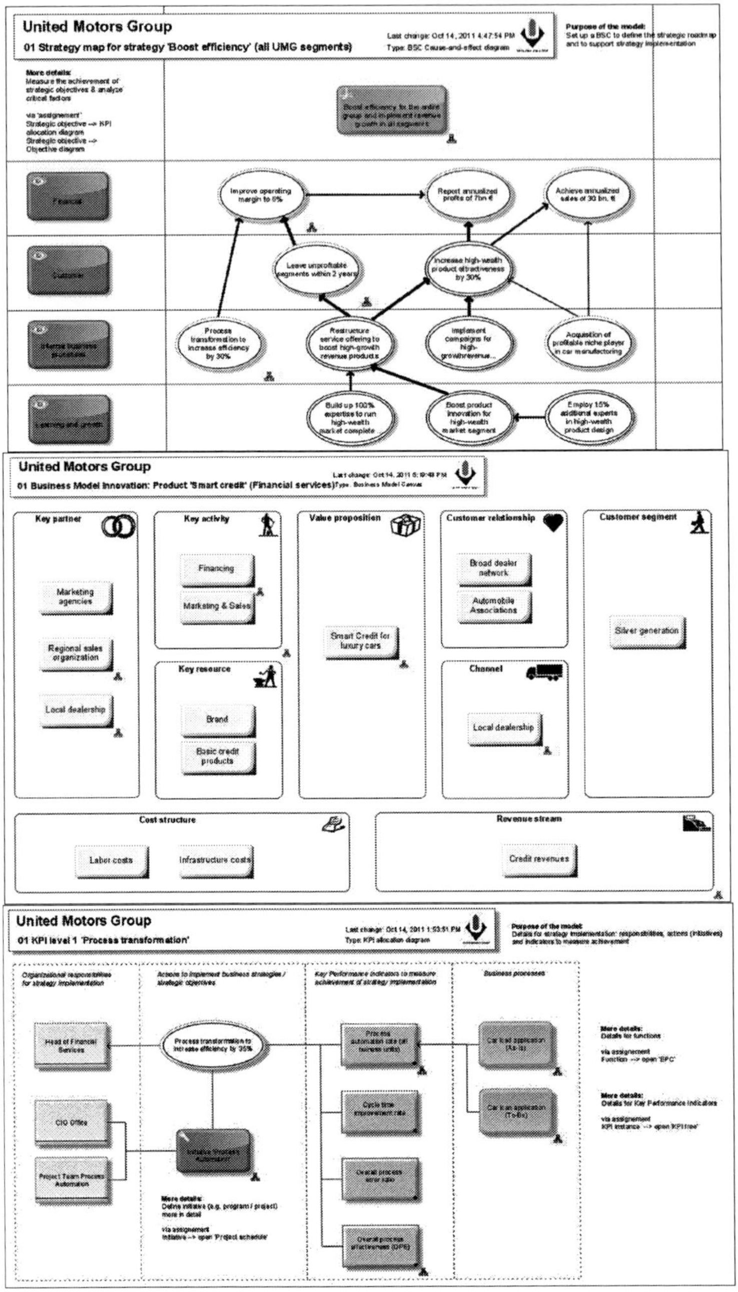

Figure 2-2: KPI Allocation Diagram & ARIS Business Strategy

A company's strategy, business processes and IT systems cannot exist in silos. They influence each other quite a lot. For instance, try to explain which processes are the core competency in your company and you will find out that the answer will have consequences for your strategy. A disconnect between the company's objectives and the daily business operation will lead to failure.

One main challenge for strategists is to define the right strategy. Another is to define the strategy the right way.

If you want to implement a successful business strategy, you need to have a method, a toolset and diagrams to support strategists in defining and implementing it. [See Figure 2-2] For example, this tool should bridge the gap between strategy definition, performance management and organizational structures. A set of diagram types helps enhance business models and plan strategies.

Use a BPA tool to:

- Perform strategic analysis and to investigate your position in the market
- Design "to-be" scenarios to help top-level managers make strategic decisions
- Benchmark your business performance compared to competitors
- Derive critical success factors for your strategy
- Design strategy models to communicate your strategy among different stakeholders
- Plan and implement a balanced scorecard as a proven management system

ARIS, for example, gives you a set of diagrams to describe your business strategy, business models, strategic objectives, critical success factors and cause-and-effect relationships. This set is called a "Business Model Canvas"—a practical tool that Alexander Osterwalder, author and speaker on business model innovation, created to help companies describe, design, challenge and ultimately invent new business models.

The canvas provides nine building blocks [Figure 2-3] that represent the core dimensions of a business model:

- Customer Segments are "... groups of people or organizations an enterprise aims to reach and serve"

- Value Propositions are the "... bundle of products and services that create value for a specific Customer Segment"
- Channels are the way "... a company communicates with and reaches its customer segments to deliver a value proposition"
- Customer Relationships represent "... types of relationships with specific customer segments"
- Revenue Streams are the "... representation of the cash a company generates from each customer segment"
- Key Resources are "... the most important assets required to make a business model work"
- Key Activities describe "... the most important things a company must do to make its business model work"
- Key Partners represents the "... network of suppliers and partners that make the business model work"
- Cost Structures cover "... all costs incurred to operate a business model"

Having designed the business strategy, you have to deliver it through your business processes. No matter what strategy approach you wish to take—SWOT analysis, using the nine building blocks or implementing a balanced scorecard—this is an important step in BPA.

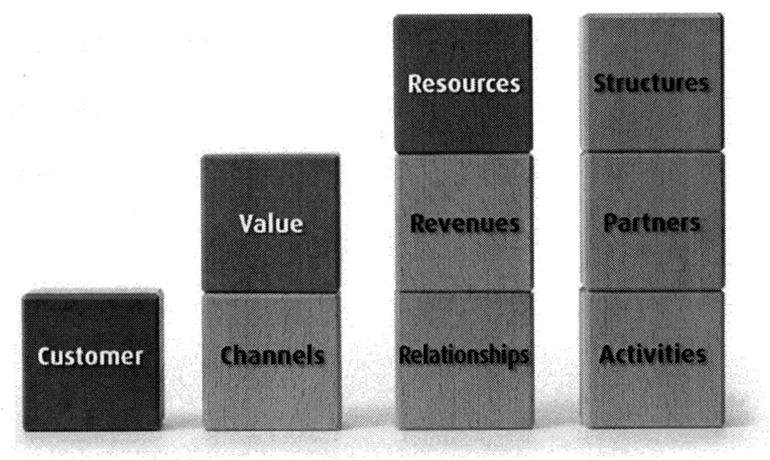

Figure 2-3: Nine building blocks of Business Model Canvas that represent the core dimensions of a business model

CREATING A GOOD PROCESS

Processes are not just something your business does. Processes are your business. Therefore you should pay attention to the design of your processes to make sure they meet your goals and are efficient.

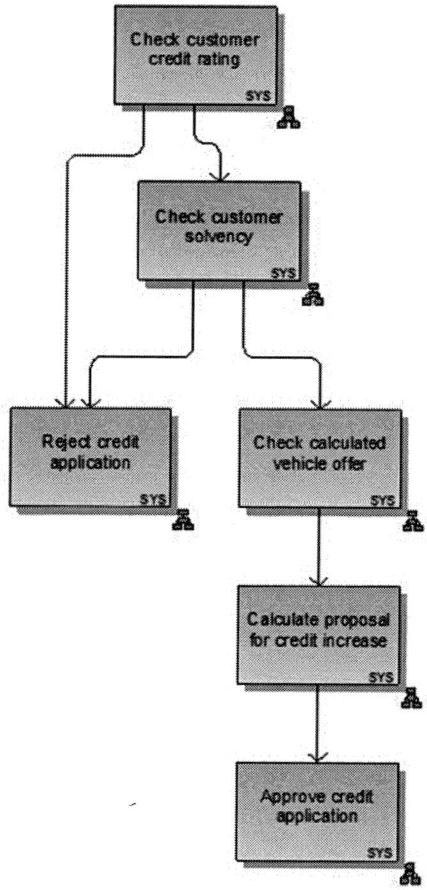

A typical business process

What Is A Process?

Simply put a process is *"the definition of the tasks and the sequence of those tasks, necessary to fulfill an objective."*

Typically a process will deliver a business objective. But the important thing is the process must deliver something (a product or service) to someone (or some organization) outside of the process and what is delivered must be of value to that person or organization. But more than that, the process must also have some value to the business itself. Usually that means someone—the customer—will pay for the product or service delivered by the process. But that is not sufficient either; the objective of the process must also align with corporate values and strategy. So a good process must:

- Deliver something of value to someone outside of the process
- Create value for the organization operating the process
- Align with corporate values and strategy

We can see that processes don't stand by themselves in isolation and, when designing or modeling a process, we need to think about more than just the process flow. A good process design must take into account three aspects:

- The definition and sequence of tasks
- The resources needed to operate them
- The environment in which they operate

Only when you consider the resources required (such as people, IT systems and services) and the environment in which the process must operate (such as laws, regulations, business policies and constraints) can you properly understand and define processes.

The Process as Transformation

Since *processes are the business*, every input into and out of the organization will be connected to a process. Processes must add value to the customer and to the business so, in fact, what they do is they transform inputs (for example, customer orders and raw materials) into outputs (such as products or services) that people will benefit from and pay for.

Visualizing the process as a transformation (and also each step in the process as a transformation) is a good way to focus the design of the process on what is important and on delivering value. [See Figure 2-4] for example, with ARIS you can model this transformation, the required resources and the controls that constrain the process.

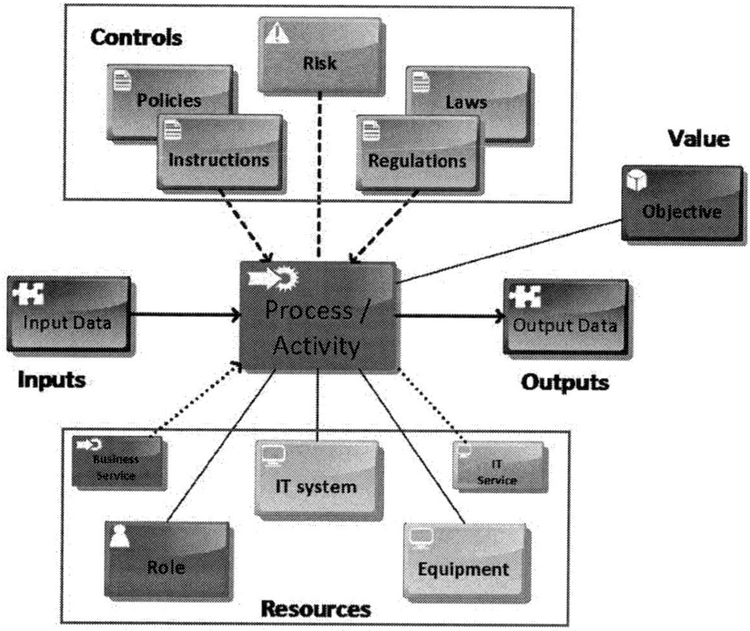

Figure 2-4: Process as Transformation

BEFORE YOU START – THE FIVE Ws AGAIN

Once you know what a process is and what elements it should contain, it is very tempting to get started on a new design or mapping an existing process. But hold on a minute! Never forget the "Five Ws of BPA" introduced earlier in this book.

Designing a process is just like any other business activity. You need to be clear about the customers you're designing the process for, what they are going to use it for and, most importantly, the benefit you expect to gain from all of this modeling work. These answers will determine the content, the format and the level of detail needed. Many organizations waste time creating inappropriate models that are never used because the modelers forgot to ask these basic questions.

So before you start modeling, ask:

- **Why are you modeling?** For instance, will the models be used for a process improvement exercise, for communicating to end users or as a specification for an IT development? Are there constraints, such as regulation, change in business structure or resource availability? How will these processes be measured and how will that affect the design? The answer to these questions will determine what sort of information you need to include and what level of detail you should go into.

- **Who are the models for?** Is there a single customer with specific requirements or are there many stakeholders throughout the business? Do they want the same things from the models and will they want to view them in the same format? Do they actually want to see the models or do they just want the results from an improvement exercise or documents derived from the process design (for example, work instructions)? Based on these answers, you may find you need to present process information in different ways to different people and with different levels of detail.
- **What are you modeling?** Are you creating a process landscape for the entire business, modeling a specific function (for example, sales) or an end-to-end process (like lead-to-cash)? Be clear about this. Often people start with one aim and get confused, lose their way and model irrelevant details. It is often sensible to start by recording a high-level enterprise process landscape and then to drill down into more detail for specific, important processes.
- **When are the models relevant?** Are you mapping the as-is process or the to-be? If it's the as-is, then are you considering what people think is happening now or what should be happening? If it's the to-be, then exactly when in the future will the process be used, what are the constraints and dependencies, and will they change? Do you actually need to model the as-is process at all? A lot can be learned from the way things are done now. But if you are embarking on an ambitious transformation project, then how things are done today may not be that relevant. Often people spend too much time on as-is modeling at the expense of the actual transformation.
- **Where will the models be used?** Will they be used by people operating the processes or just by process architects and designers? In what format will people want the designs (for example, on a Web portal or on paper)? Do they just want to look at them or directly use the models (to directly automate the process, for example)? Do the processes need to be shared with third parties or conform to any modeling standards?

We will talk about the "how" in a later section.

Standards Are Key

Once you know why you are modeling, what sort of detail is required and how it needs to be presented, you can define your modeling standards. You need standards to:

- Ensure models created by different teams can link together and form a corporate asset
- Ensure your process models can be easily understood by all
- Make the design tools simple to use
- Reduce training costs and facilitate outsourcing and recruiting
- Enable designs to transfer to other tools for implementation and automation

Many people use drawing tools to document their processes and invent their own templates and symbols. The meaning of these may be clear to them but are often unintelligible to others. Hence, they don't form part of a corporate asset.

The How – Creating the Model

Now you're ready to start creating the process model. [See Figure 2-5] but how do you start and where? The best approach is to tackle it in three phases that match the three aspects of a process design described earlier:

- Outline the process flow
- Allocate resources
- Map to the environment

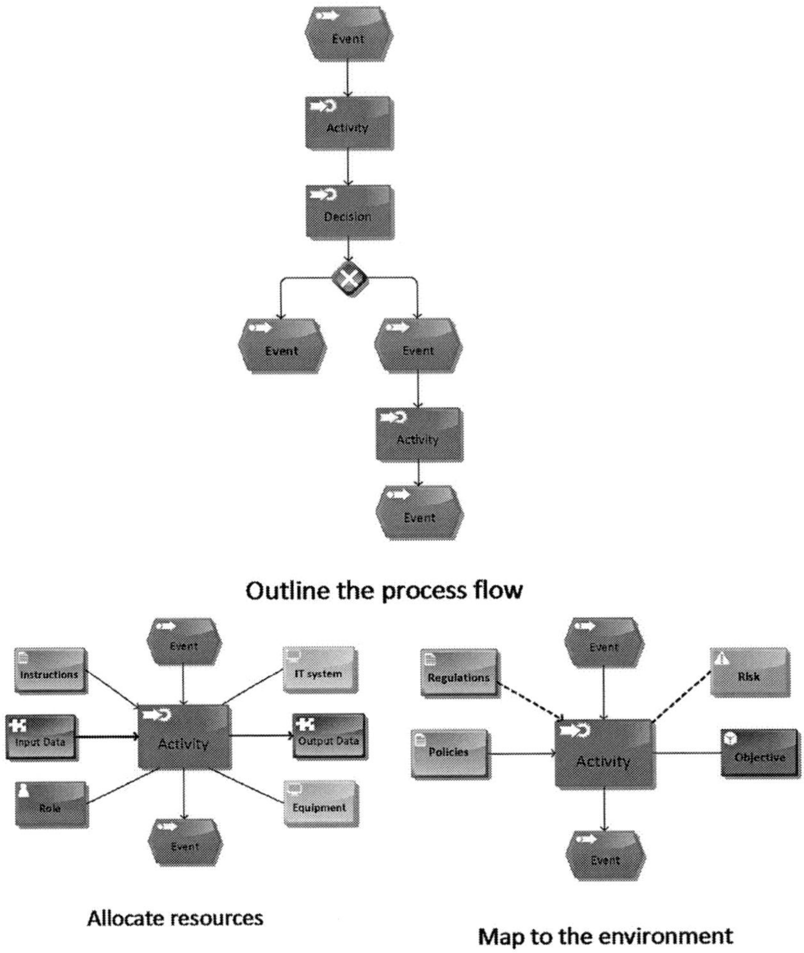

Figure 2-5: Creating the Model

These phases are not rigid. In practice, use them as needed to add more detail to your design. Start by documenting the process flow and think about:

- What triggers the process?
- Is there just one trigger or are there other dependencies?
- What decisions are made by the process?
- What failures can occur and do you need to cater for them?

Don't make the mistake of just modeling the "happy path," that is, what happens when things go right. The most testing times for your organization, and the ones on which your customers will judge you, is when problems occur. Manage these well, and you will create customer loyalty.

Some failures or alternative scenarios are important to the business (that is, they incur costs, affect customer satisfaction or contravene regulation, for example) and must be modeled. Others may be less important and can be managed by a generic fault handling or escalation process.

Creating the flow is best done with one or two subject matter experts. Once you have the outline of the process flow, then walk through it step by step with the experts and ask them:

- Who does the tasks and what skills do they need?
- What information or documents are required?
- What IT systems support the task?
- What business services does the task require or what IT services automate the task?
- What equipment or specialized resources are needed?

As you add this information to your model, you will almost certainly find that you need to alter the process flow. You may find there are additional steps required such as, gathering necessary information or checking that the right equipment is available. It's only when you add this additional information that you will get a realistic design.

Also remember most processes operating in the services industry transform data (for example, a customer order for broadband into network configuration data). So your design must consider the data flowing through the process so it will be an accurate and effective operational process.

If you are designing the process to be automated using re-usable IT services, then you need to establish the library of services beforehand and allocate these to the activities. This step is often performed by a business analyst who defines the required business capability for an activity and maps it to one or more business services. Later, a process engineer identifies the specific IT service(s) that deliver the capability. To achieve high levels of re-use, it may be necessary to adjust the business process design to make use of existing IT services rather than request new ones to be created.

The final phase is about making sure that the process is fit-for-purpose within the business environment and checking that it meets your customer's requirements. Look at the process and ask:

- Does the process add value to the customer and the organization?
- Does each step in the process add value or fulfill an essential business function (for example, health and safety)?
- Does the process align with corporate strategy, the enterprise architecture and design policies?
- Are there provisions in place to measure the performance of the process? (It may be necessary to add process activities to capture appropriate metrics)
- Does the process take into account relevant regulations, risks, business policies and branding? Are required audit mechanisms in place?
- Will the customer's experience of the process be a good one and has it been measured and benchmarked?

How Do You Know When You Have Finished?

This is an important question and the phrase to keep in mind is: Don't model the universe!

The scope of the process design and the amount of detail you need should have been set by considering the Five Ws. You should know what your customers expect from the process, what they are going to do with it and what formats they want. In particular, the level of detail required will be affected by issues such as:

- What affects the customer?
- What generates revenue?
- What incurs cost?
- What is affected by regulations?
- Where are the risks?
- What information do people need to do their jobs?

If the detail in your model doesn't seem to fit any of these categories, then check if it's really needed. If you are not sure if your process is complete, check what your customer asked for.

Verifying & Validating Your Process

Your process design is now complete. But is it correct? There are two categories of things to consider:

Verification - Does your process meet the customer's requirements?

Validation – Is your process what the business actually needs?

Often what the customer asked for is not what he or she actually wanted. That's either because the customer couldn't articulate clearly what he or she wanted or because things have now changed. It's the process designer's job to verify that the process is what the business needs. You should check the process to make sure it is:

- Effective - Does it do what it is supposed to? It must be simple and make life better for all concerned. It must demonstrably deliver value to customers.
- Efficient - It must use available resources to best effect and be devoid of waste, unnecessary steps, multiple hand-overs and other wasteful characteristics.
- Relevant - It must carry out a task that is important to the business and align with business strategy and corporate policies.
- Valid - It should work, describe the business scenarios most frequently encountered and have a fallback route for exceptions.
- Usable - It should be realistic, easy to understand, employ the appropriate amount of detail and be available to those who need to use it.
- Re-usable - It should employ common components described by the enterprise architecture and be available for other designers to re-use.
- Managed - The process must have an owner who will sign-off on the design, ensuring it aligns with requirements and business strategy.
- Measured - The process should have measures "designed-in" so that the process owner can monitor and manage it.

Avoiding the Pitfalls

By following these BPA principles, you should avoid most of the pitfalls described in Chapter 1. An important thing to keep in mind is: A process model is not the real thing. It's just a representation of how you intend the business to operate.

The process design will have a certain level of detail and a particular viewpoint. It will have been created at a specific moment in time. Process design is all about ensuring that the viewpoint, detail and timing are what the business needs. Even when the process is designed well, many people fail to communicate the process to the right people. The most important thing to keep in mind is: A process model is just a model. To transform the business, you must implement and manage the process.

IMPROVING THE PROCESS

Process improvement is a key activity in BPA. This activity improves existing processes or improves your designs for new processes. Important tools for process improvement include:

- Process analysis
- Process simulation
- Process improvement methods

Let's take a look using ARIS as an example.

Process Analysis

ARIS enables a static analysis of process design. Typically static process analysis covers:

- Organizational handoffs - Does the process move from department-to-department or role-to-role? Minimizing organizational handoffs speeds up process performance and reduces opportunity for error.
- Media breaks - Does the information the process uses and transforms exist in different formats or sources (such as paper, fax or e-mail)? Manual or automated conversion can lead to errors.
- System breaks - Is the end-to-end process implemented by multiple IT systems? Reducing the number of systems and interfaces reduces costs and can improve performance.
- Value - Does each activity add value to the customer or the business? If not, why have it? If it doesn't have value, but is essential (to support processes, such as human resources, safety or auditing, for example) is it done efficiently?

Process Simulation

Do you have process bottlenecks? How is your resource utilization? What are the cost implications? With a dynamic business process simulator that lets you quickly analyze and improve your business processes, you can easily answer these questions.

You can simulate processes to try out different resource profiles, change throughput rates or make changes to the process and quickly see the likely impact. This helps improve process efficiency and cost effectiveness and reduces the risks of introducing new processes by allowing you to experiment without direct operational impact. Different resource policies, shift calendars and priorities can simulate realistic resource deployments and throughputs can be modeled with a variety of different distributions and time allocations.

Process Improvement Methods

Tools and techniques for process improvement are best deployed systematically as part of a process improvement method such as Lean, Kaizen and Six Sigma.

ARIS provides full support for the Design for Six Sigma DMAIC lifecycle (Define-Measure-Analyze-Improve-Control). It has a variety of model types [see Figure 2-6] that range from scope definition (SIPOC), identifying problem areas (fishbone diagrams), defining measurable critical success factors (CTX diagrams) and reporting in RASCI charts to show Responsible/Accountable /Supportive/Consulted/Informed roles.

Value Stream Modeling (VSM) is a Lean technique used to define all the activities and information flows required to create a product from its raw materials. VSM can be used for modeling manufacturing industry supply chains but also service-related industries. It is complementary to the "process as a transformation" concept introduced earlier.

The VSM model supports industry standard symbols, can calculate the process timeline and generate Kaizen and process efficiency reports that show losses due to downtime, inefficiencies and quality issues. It also can evaluate the need for efficiency improvements. You can focus on the whole end-to-end value stream while improving individual process quality. Using ARIS, you can integrate VSMs within your other process architecture (such as Event-driven Process Chains (EPCs), Value-added chains and Supplier, Input, Process, Output, Customer SIPOC).

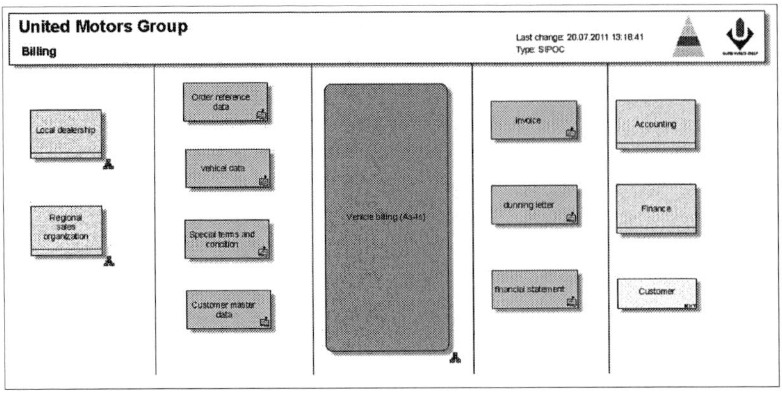

SIPOC

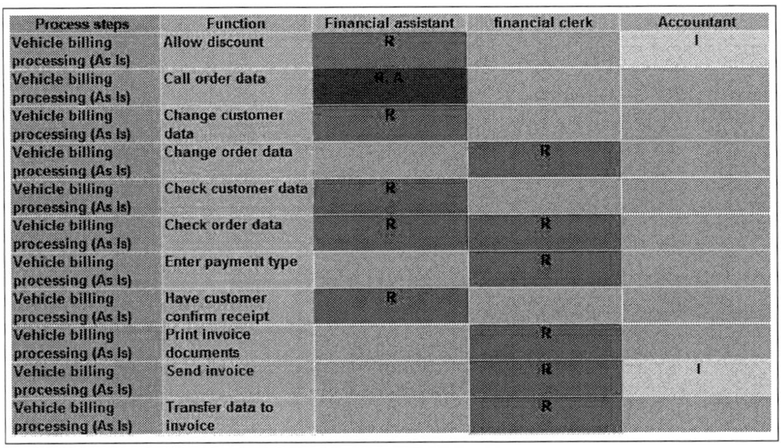

Process steps	Function	Financial assistant	financial clerk	Accountant
Vehicle billing processing (As Is)	Allow discount	R		I
Vehicle billing processing (As Is)	Call order data	R, A		
Vehicle billing processing (As Is)	Change customer data	R		
Vehicle billing processing (As Is)	Change order data		R	
Vehicle billing processing (As Is)	Check customer data	R		
Vehicle billing processing (As Is)	Check order data	R	R	
Vehicle billing processing (As Is)	Enter payment type		R	
Vehicle billing processing (As Is)	Have customer confirm receipt	R		
Vehicle billing processing (As Is)	Print invoice documents		R	
Vehicle billing processing (As Is)	Send invoice		R	I
Vehicle billing processing (As Is)	Transfer data to invoice		R	

RASCI

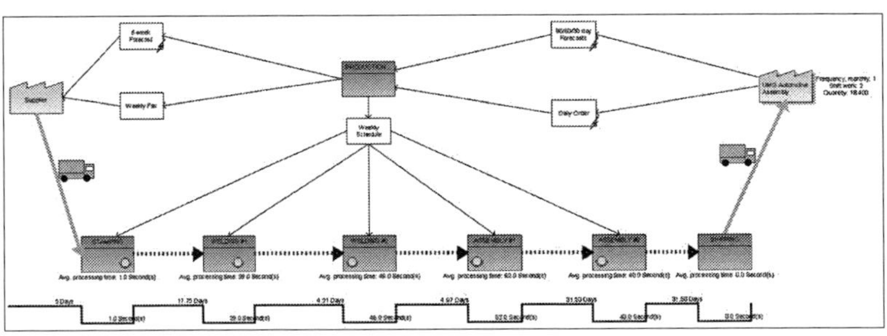

Value Stream Map

Figure 2-6: Process Improvement Methods

The main pillar of Six Sigma is Statistical Process Control (SPC). It can be directly implemented by ARIS Process Intelligence and integrated with MINITAB®, the market-leading software for SPC analysis projects allowing graphical analysis, such as boxplot and control charts.

Realizing the importance of these industry standard improvement methodologies we have built them into the ARIS product. All the information is captured in the ARIS repository so it becomes a corporate asset.

PROCESS GOVERNANCE

Process improvement programs are normally not a "one man show" but a common project for different stakeholders, such as the CIO, process owners, business analysts and process engineers [see Figure 2-7]. To ensure first-class process management, you need to establish effective end-to-end governance of your processes.

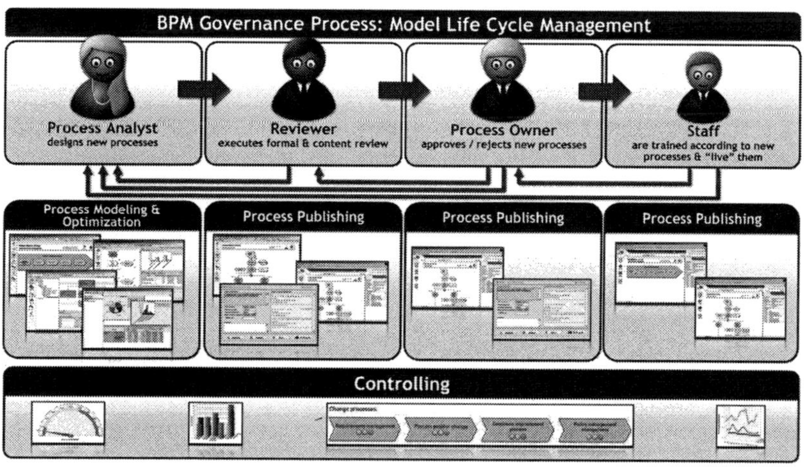

Figure 2-7: Process Governance

Process governance is a set of policies and processes that define the way the organization's business processes are managed. Key elements of good process governance include transparency, responsibility, flexibility, accountability, commitment to the organization's business goals and fast realization through automation. A good BPA solution offers governance using a model-driven workflow approach. Governance processes are modeled just like any other process. They can be represented with various levels of detail, such as value chains and EPCs. This sequential representation is enhanced by a role view, which assigns process steps to the relevant employees.

The key benefits of process governance are:

- Enhanced process transparency, quality and flexibility
- Model-based approach ensuring that the executed process corresponds to the modeled process
- Process changes and ad hoc collaboration becomes possible without IT support
- Automated task lists and escalation mechanisms
- End-to-end process control
- Measurement and visualization of process KPIs

Achieve end-to-end control with flexible and efficient process management.

COMMUNICATION & PUBLISHING

Having your business processes designed, analyzed and mapped to your business strategy is wonderful. But if you do not communicate what you achieved, your efforts will fail. [See Figure 2-8]

To share process information within your company, you need a flexible, low-cost process portal tool that guarantees availability of process information or IT architectures.

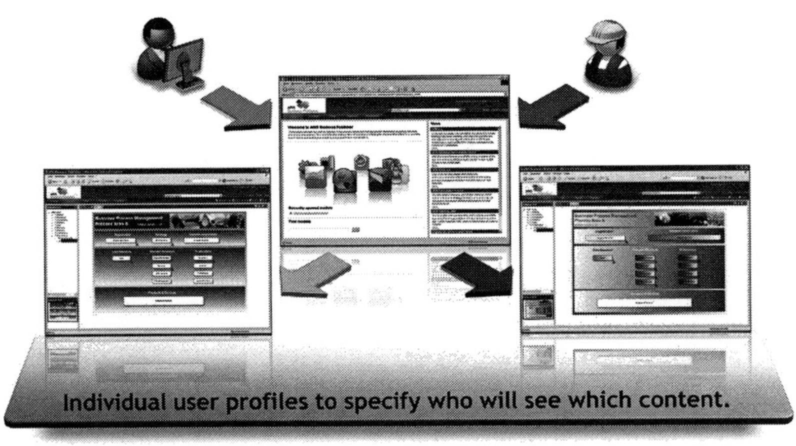

Figure 2-8: Communication & Publishing

With strong BPA software, such as ARIS, you can:

- Publish process knowledge or IT environments via web portals for easy access
- Control who gets what knowledge via rights or role-based access
- Customize process portals to your corporate "look and feel"
- Integrate seamlessly with SAP®, enterprise portals as well as Microsoft® Office® products and document management systems
- Run reports company-wide

A process transformation project is only complete when your employees have the knowledge they need by getting them the right information in the right context.

GETTING IN SYNC WITH IT

BPA helps companies to design their enterprise including: business and IT processes and their complex flow and decision logic; organizational responsibilities and structures; technical and business requirements; related data flow and architectures; systems; services; and much more. This is done for the purpose of documenting, analyzing, simulating and publishing.

With Enterprise BPM, we focus on three different kinds of business and IT alignment:

- Model-to-Execute (M2E), the seamless integration of your business process models and the IT automation and execution of those models.
- Process-driven SAP, the direct link to your SAP systems
- Enterprise Architecture (EA) Management

Having successfully implemented a BPA project, you still face the challenge of closing the gap between business and technical/IT processes. In most organizations, business and IT processes are completely separated. There is no communication, translation or alignment of business and IT.

This is one of the reasons Software AG developed M2E, a seamless, automated and governed integration of process models and automation. Everything your BPA project achieves for the business side can be shared with IT in an easy way.

Process-driven SAP is also part of Enterprise BPM or can be part of a BPA project. But how can ARIS help during an SAP project?

For starters, the models are easy to understand, relevant to the business, and also are a language to translate business requirements into system requirements. Understanding the interrelations of a company and all its assets and processes in a modeled format can bring simplicity to a complex SAP project. Documentation should not only be the single point of communication at the beginning of the project, but also stays relevant and accurate throughout and long after the project is completed. This can only be realized if the process documentation is interlinked with the application lifecycle tool, SAP Solution Manager.

But technical integration is only one key point. Process-driven SAP management is a combination of tools, content and methodology.

With Process-driven SAP management, you can lower your total cost of ownership by reducing project times and simplifying the customization process.

To learn more, please download the white paper called "Process-Driven SAP Management" at www.softwareag.com/resources.

EA management is the topic of the next chapter. So, stay tuned to learn about our fully integrated solution for EA management that enables you to:

- Analyze, optimize, plan and manage your enterprise
- Synchronize IT change with business needs
- Create the right roadmap for your business products, services and ICT solutions
- Harmonize how ICT supports your business
- Define and track your enterprise-wide standards
- Optimize your IT budget and risk management

EBPM Success – Cargolux

cargolux

500% ROI

Cargolux delivers savings potential 500% higher than its BPM investment.

Process improvements took off at Europe's largest all-cargo carrier, operating 14 Boeing 747 freighters in a worldwide network—all thanks to analyzing logistics, staff utilization and data workflows. The ARIS Platform provided Cargolux complete visualization and modeling of business processes, identified disruptive factors and uncovered potential areas for savings. More than 180 improvements were identified with project costs comprising only 20 percent of projected savings.

> *"The ARIS Platform enabled us to conduct a process analysis, pinpoint weaknesses in individual processes, and identify the potential cost benefits ..."*
>
> Henrik Ambak
> VP, Ground Services & Commercial IT,
> Cargolux

For more examples of successes with Enterprise BPM, please go to www.softwareag.com/resources.

EBPM Success – Aleris

Aleris Europe

30% reduced costs

Aleris speeds up process time and rounds out cost savings at 30 percent.

Aleris wanted to reduce process time and simplify processes. Using ARIS, the aluminum manufacturer analyzed existing processes and costs, designed new target processes and estimated new process expenses. Benefits of using the ARIS tool included a 30 percent reduction in costs over time. The order confirmation process is now twice as fast, and ROI is excellent, thanks to project costs of 36 percent based on annual savings.

> *"Thanks to the achieved process optimization we can now meet customer requirements faster, more reliably and more accurately."*
>
> Detlev Weckmüller
> Director Supply Chain,
> Aleris Europe

For more examples of successes with Enterprise BPM, please go to www.softwareag.com/resources.

CHAPTER 3

ENTERPRISE ARCHITECTURE (EA) MANAGEMENT—Getting IT on Track with Your Processes and Your Business

INTRODUCTION

Are your IT investments in line with business objectives and processes? If you want to run a successful Enterprise BPM program, you'll need to get them all on the same track.

In fact, with the right approach to Enterprise Architecture (EA) Management, you'll be able to deliver high-quality IT solutions faster to meet business demands. Business managers will understand and value IT investments because IT will help drive process improvement—and business success.

Sound interesting? In this chapter, you'll learn how EA has changed from a very technology-focused IT discipline—with few links to the business—to a strategic management discipline that ensures IT supports business growth and success.

You'll see how EA can make a vital contribution to a large organization. EA is not about creating models and architectures for their own sake. It's about using these structures to serve the needs of the business and support the long-term business strategy.

EA management can help you reach your goals with Enterprise BPM. So let's explore it!

What is EA?

In short, IT can be a real driver for business success. Here's why.

IT environments have become more complex and extensive due to business growth. For example, mergers and acquisitions have created redundant systems and applications across many enterprises. At the same time, markets have changed rapidly, and innovation for both technology and business continue to boom.

To survive amid such change, enterprises have to be very adaptive with more flexible IT support. CIOs are forced to transform the IT landscape to meet the demands of a future-proof organization. As a consequence, IT departments are no longer seen as financial burdens. Instead, they're proving to be beneficial business partners. By bringing value through technology, IT becomes a key driver for day-to-day business success, increasing both operating efficiency and top-line growth.

Still, in some companies, IT departments struggle to understand exactly what the business wants or which goals they are trying to achieve. Consequently, IT is often accused of not delivering what was demanded. Timelines of IT projects often are not in sync with the strategic goals of the business. This missing link between business and IT is nothing new. In fact, it has driven EA from the start.

EA in a Nutshell

Gartner defines EA as "... the process of translating business vision and strategy into effective enterprise change by creating, communicating, and improving the key principles and models that describe the enterprise's future state and enable its evolution."

An EA describes the complex system of corporate IT resources and pinpoints the link between a company's business processes, applications, data and infrastructure. [See Figure 3-1] To understand this complex system, multiple perspectives must be taken into account, spanning the overall enterprise view at a highly abstract level and detailed views of departments and physical systems.

Without the analysis, planning and transformation of the different elements of the four layers as shown in Figure 3-1, the optimization of the operational business and the infrastructure becomes a shot in the dark—a journey into the unknown without a road map and a clear destination.

EA is neither just an IT topic nor a business discipline. It is a combined approach of both sides. For a while, it was treated as a discipline for IT managers only. But today it is instrumental in connecting the business strategy top-down to the operational level. EA is a medium for the dialog between business and IT.

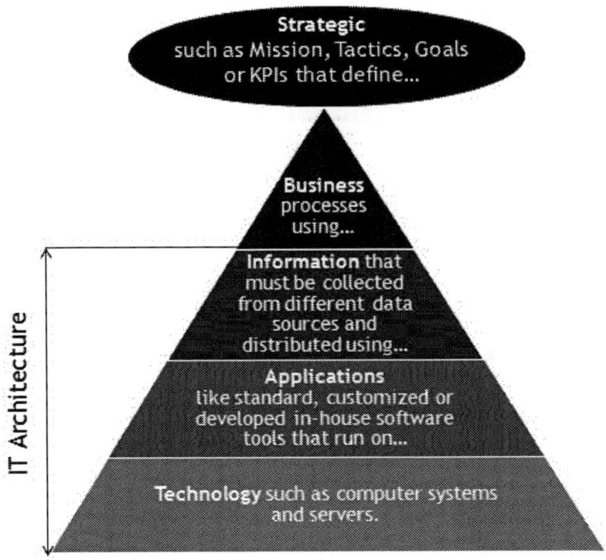

Figure 3-1: The four Architecture Layers of EA

EA in the Context of Enterprise BPM

EA plays a crucial role in the context of Enterprise BPM. Historically, EA and BPA have evolved independently of each other. However, over recent years, they've become tightly connected. BPA is a management and planning discipline, in which business users, business architects and business process analysts work together and collaborate on the design and improvement of business processes to drive business transformation. Consequently, it's becoming the starting point for process execution within BPM initiatives.

The overall goal is to force operational excellence and business process agility to improve the performance of the enterprise. However, achieving these objectives takes the right applications and technologies to design, execute and monitor business processes. But which technologies should be picked? Which applications are the ones to rely on? What's the IT roadmap, the future IT landscape and how much does it cost? This is where EA comes into play.

As described previously, EA is a management and planning discipline, in which enterprise architects, IT architects and other stakeholders from business and IT collaborate on the transformation of the IT landscape to actively support and facilitate the transformation of the business. EA management shares the goal of enabling business change to operationalize enterprise strategy, and it's consequently another entry point in the Enterprise BPM lifecycle.

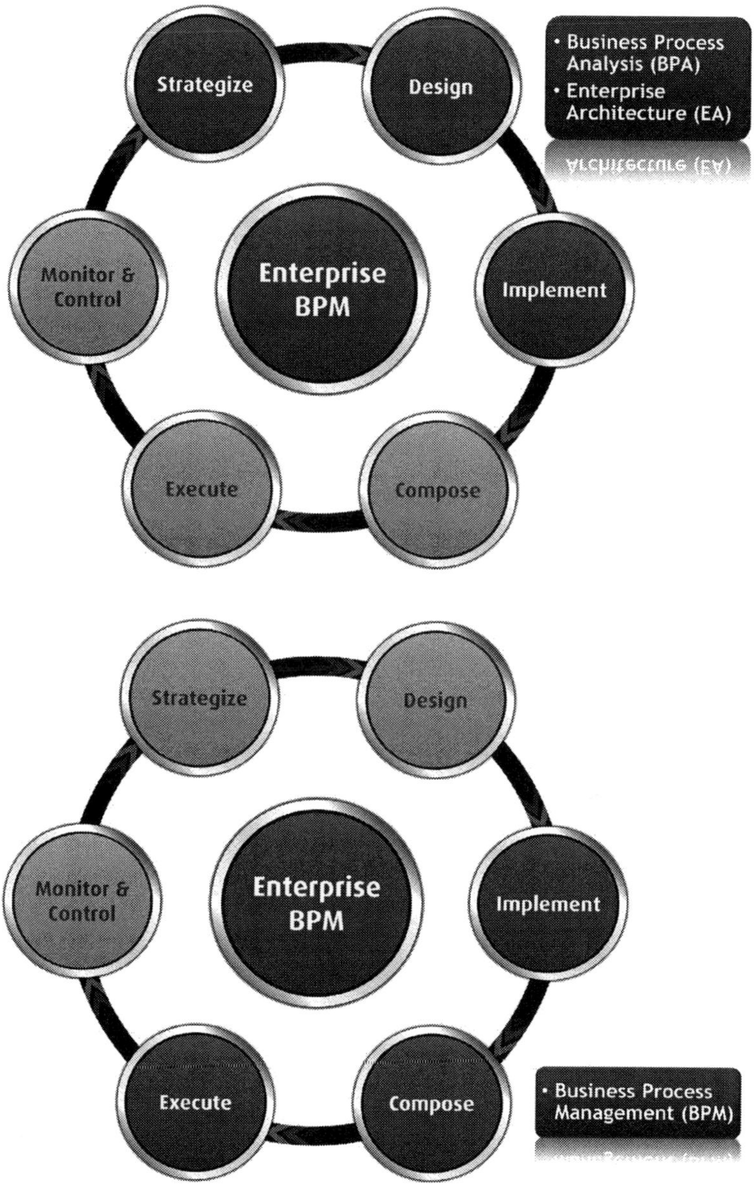

Figure 3-2: The role of Enterprise Architecture in Enterprise BPM

But what's the use of a great idea if no one creates a plan to realize it? Combining the holistic planning aspects of EA with the process and optimization focus of BPA and BPM guarantees that constant business improvement will actually happen. [See Figure 3-2]

Here are the top four results of this winning combination:

- EA provides answers about what exactly must be done to transform the IT landscape and close the gap between business and IT strategy and its execution
- EA needs the business context to plan architectural change, and this naturally includes BPA and is one of the reasons why these two topics converge at some levels
- BPM projects run in the context of architectural guidelines, principles and technical references and are subjected to IT budget constraints that actually are managed within an EA
- Within the IT organization, BPA/BPM projects are planned through an EA; likewise, EA projects—for example, application harmonization plans—can result from BPA initiatives that become reality through the Enterprise BPM lifecycle

It's essential not to forget the people actually working and collaborating within the lifecycle of Enterprise BPM. Architectures, timelines and plans created in EA are directly linked to budgets and projects that have to be approved by managers. Decisions have to be underpinned by facts. Business people have to define and pass their requirements properly to IT. IT itself has to justify investments by documenting the outcomes and values to the business.

This only can happen by establishing comprehensive governance processes that link stakeholders across BPA, BPM and EA. With the right governance processes in place, you can make sure every stakeholder has the same overall objective: Business Process Excellence.

Why Invest In An EA Program?

EA is driven by the top concerns of CIOs and business leaders. They call for flexible organizations, strategy planning and cost reduction through better efficiency. An EA must be able to support these top business concerns. To accomplish this mission, business-related objectives must be translated into EA objectives, scenarios and use cases.

CIOs are between the "devil and the deep blue sea." On the one hand, they need to keep IT costs under control. On the other hand, they are forced to get more value out of IT with less budget and deliver better ROI to the business with reduced risk.

Enterprise architects have to convert these CIO pain points into EA use cases. For example, they need to:

- Find redundancies within the IT landscape
- Identify business-critical systems
- Detect which applications can be eliminated without a negative impact

To do so, they need one thing as a foundation: transparency. Getting that is not as easy as it sounds. Organizations need a transparent view—not only about the IT itself but also how IT interrelates with the business.

This is crucial to:

- Derive requirements directly from business processes
- Provide a deeper insight into the alignment between business demand and IT capability
- Deliver better high-quality solutions to meet business demands
- Communicate the value of IT investments
- Provide business justification for IT decisions
- Articulate how IT can drive business strategy and, thus, actively support business success

But still, in most organizations, business and IT processes are separated completely. There is no communication, translation or alignment. So there is no way to gain a clear insight into the complex enterprise.

Business Benefits

So considering all of these challenges, how can EA management help? In the end, an EA can only be successful—and worth the investment—if real value is provided to the IT and business organization. Here are the top four business benefits you get from an EA management program:

Better IT transparency - This is the foundation of a successful EA and, at the same time, the biggest challenge. The strategic orientation of the application system landscape, the associated coordination and standardization, and the control of IT budgets based on it require the entire IT landscape to be highly transparent. Heterogeneous information management, the often redundant data storage, and a lack of transparency between IT strategy and operations throw a monkey wrench into the works of an IT organization.

Reduced IT cost and complexity - Corporate growth typically goes hand in hand with an increasingly complex IT environment. Mergers and acquisitions extend the redundancy while shrinking system lifecycles and changing business environments necessitate more flexible IT support. It becomes increasingly difficult to identify business-critical systems, and cost-cutting targets prove elusive. The only viable strategy is to align IT structures with business objectives and processes, thereby enabling sustained improvements and a significant reduction in complexity and of cost of developing, maintaining and upgrading IT systems.

Improved agility and flexibility - IT is challenged to react quickly and flexibly to meet business demands in the face of increased technical complexity and tight budget constraints. Transforming IT into a responsive and flexible construct can not only speed up time to market but also establish the foundation to becoming a high-performance organization.

Alignment of business with IT - Very often, IT and business professionals are unable to align their activities because of differences in objectives, culture and incentives. As a consequence, IT is still the infamous "black box" with no transparency into how IT investments really support business challenges and needs. The alignment of business and IT is closely associated with initiatives to improve the business value of IT investments. In addition to that, the need to operationalize IT strategy—which itself must be aligned with the business strategy—is another reason why the integration between business and IT is essential to support business growth. The result of the alignment is that business transformation goes hand in hand with the transformation of IT.

How to Get Clear Insight into Your Complex Enterprise

The Four A's of an EA

Typically an EA is described using four different architectures:

1. Business architecture
2. Information architecture
3. Application architecture
4. Technical architecture

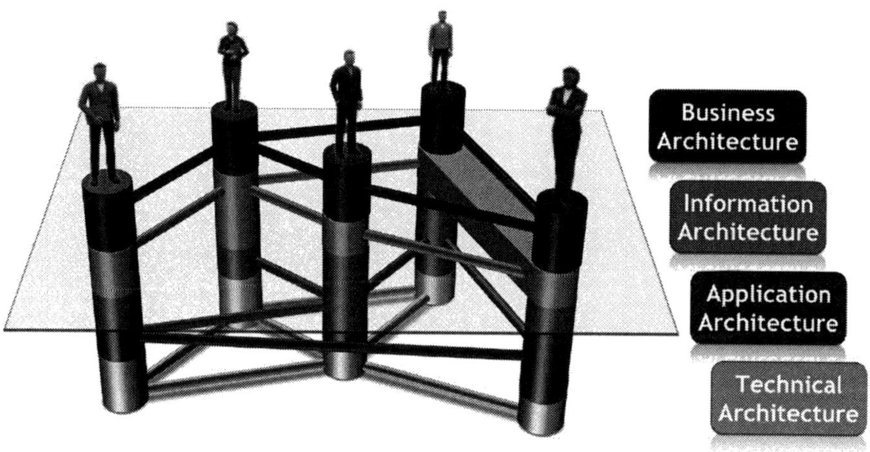

Figure 3-3: The Four A's of an EA

Only by documenting and designing these four architectures [See Figure 3-3] will you get a holistic view of your organization, including processes and strategy as well as used technologies, data and applications:

- The **business architecture** defines business strategies and describes organizational structures and business processes
- The **application architecture** describes the services and application systems that support the business processes
- The **information architecture** describes the business objects and data that are exchanged between process participants and applications
- The **technical architecture** is used to describe the technologies and IT components used by the applications

This type of description highlights the impact of business process changes on the associated applications. System redundancy can be detected and new IT requirements identified. Similarly, business processes affected by application shutdowns and technology changes can be easily identified.

As noted previously, the need for transparency is still one of the biggest challenges within organizations. This is because the many pieces of the IT landscape, business processes and the strategies they relate to are documented in different places with different tools at different times. In fact, sometimes they are not fully documented.

For this reason, the methods and integrated tools used for EA must create a structure that's fully synchronized with process management and covers all four architectures in one common repository. Additionally, it must have the ability to comply with requirements of different user roles, perfectly integrating all stakeholders and support them in their daily business.

For example, Software AG's EA solution includes the market-leading EA tool used by customers worldwide to centrally analyze, plan and transform their business processes, applications, technologies and data. It combines cutting-edge BPM technologies with global EA standards.

EA Roles

A company-wide EA project requires many people to be involved from all across the enterprise. There are many different roles and responsibilities. Sometimes the same person can have multiple roles. Additionally, depending on his or her responsibility, each stakeholder has certain expectations, use cases and demands concerning an EA. This, for example, can go from specific IT landscape views for an enterprise architect to all-in-one dashboards for the CIO.

For the success of the program, it's essential to:

- Define a clear set of roles
- Provide an explicit description
- Distinguish between the different responsibilities

Focus on the function a person has within the EA program, rather than tampering with job titles. Define mission-critical departments within your organization and consider areas that constitute the competitive advantage of your company.

To address the different users of an EA tool properly and actively support them in their daily business, typically we divide all stakeholders in three major groups:

- **Architecture roles** - Enterprise architects, business analysts and process owners are examples of roles that use the EA tool to design, architect, plan and transform. [See Figure 3-4]

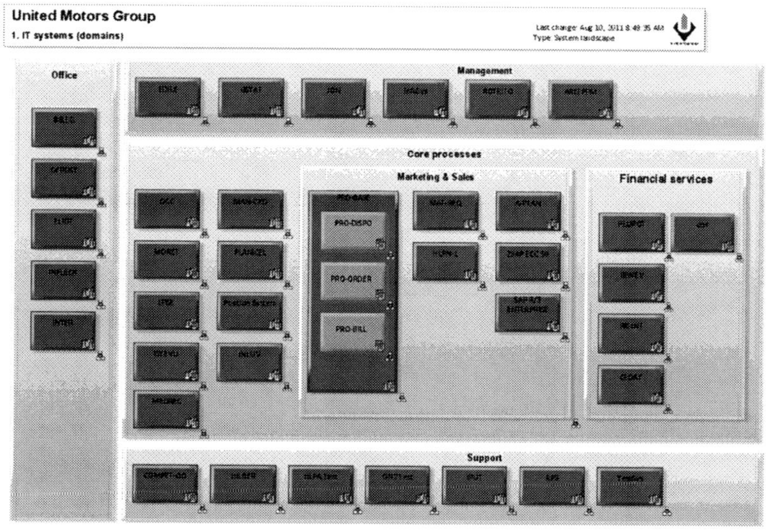

Figure 3-4: Application Landscape

- **Supporter roles** - System managers, technology architects, employees from the legal department and members of the work council are examples of roles that provide data and information about the IT landscape within an IT inventory as an information foundation for the architecture roles. [See Figure 3-5]

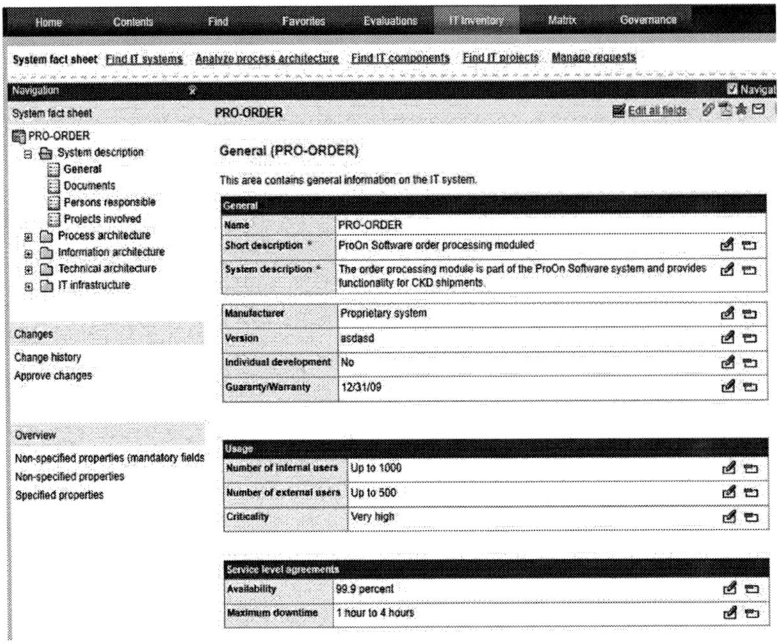

Figure 3-5: IT Inventory

- **Management roles** - CIOs, CTOs, heads of IT and project managers are examples of roles who use EA information to analyze, evaluate, control and make decisions. [See Figure 3-6]

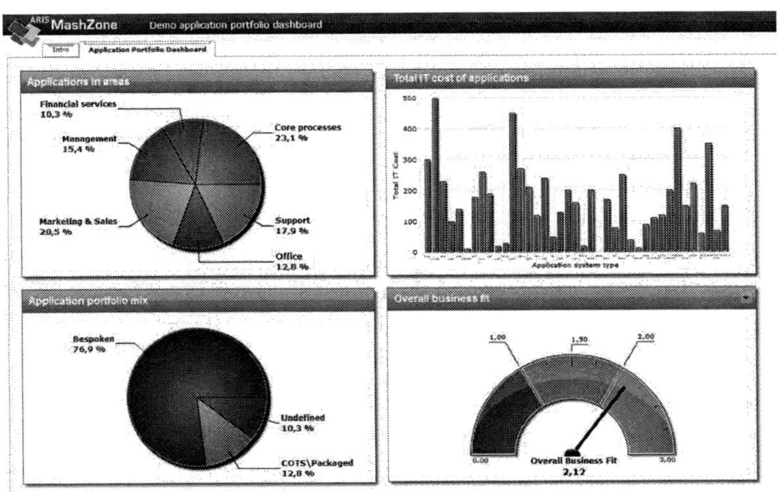

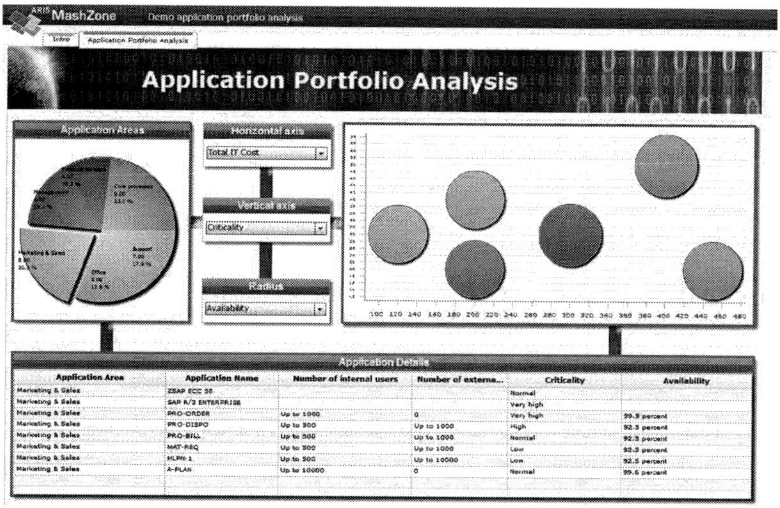

Figure 3-6: Management dashboard

Stakeholder-oriented viewpoints are the key to success. So identify your stakeholders' needs and define the appropriate EA goals including the results that matter for them.

Seek out the right people for the respective goal. Give them everything they need to feel comfortable, and let them develop their know-how to bring out the best in your stakeholders.

Use Cases and Frameworks

Do you know you need EA but you don't know where to start? That's ok because EA is a big and broad topic, so just pick a single use case that's highly visible and focus on just one goal you want to achieve.

In general, EA encompasses several generic use cases. These are completed through industry-specific models, EA frameworks and methodologies as well as templates for the industrialization of IT.

Based on years of experience in EA projects, we identified the most typical use cases:

- **IT Strategy**
  IT Strategy is derived from business strategy, not vice versa. The focus is on the value IT can deliver to the business, because IT is a means to an end. To improve and deliver business value, IT executives have to analyze not only the application and service

portfolio but also the IT organization and the corresponding IT management processes. EA enables this process by performing strategic analysis, benchmarking of the business performance compared to competitors or by improving performance planning and implementation using Balanced Scorecards. By defining the right strategy, you will achieve operational excellence. [See Figure 3-7]

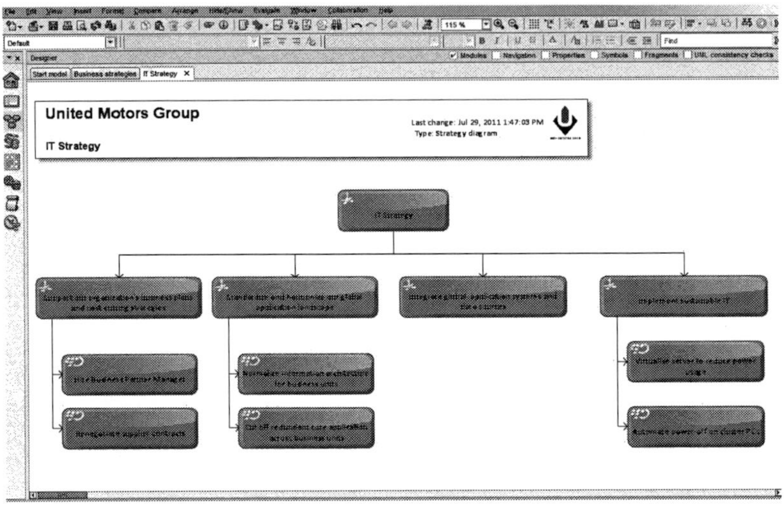

Figure 3-7: IT Strategy

- **IT Architecture Management**
  IT Architecture Management is a core use case within EA Management. It's all about harmonizing and standardizing not only the application landscape but also the technology stack of a company, bearing the strategy in mind to transform a system-oriented IT landscape into a service-oriented one. To drive these initiatives, IT architects are defining, composing and establishing reference architectures, architectural patterns and principles as well as re-usable architectural building blocks. At the same time, appropriate analytics as well as control mechanisms and governance processes are fundamental for IT architects to achieve their goals. [See Figure 3-8 and 3-9]

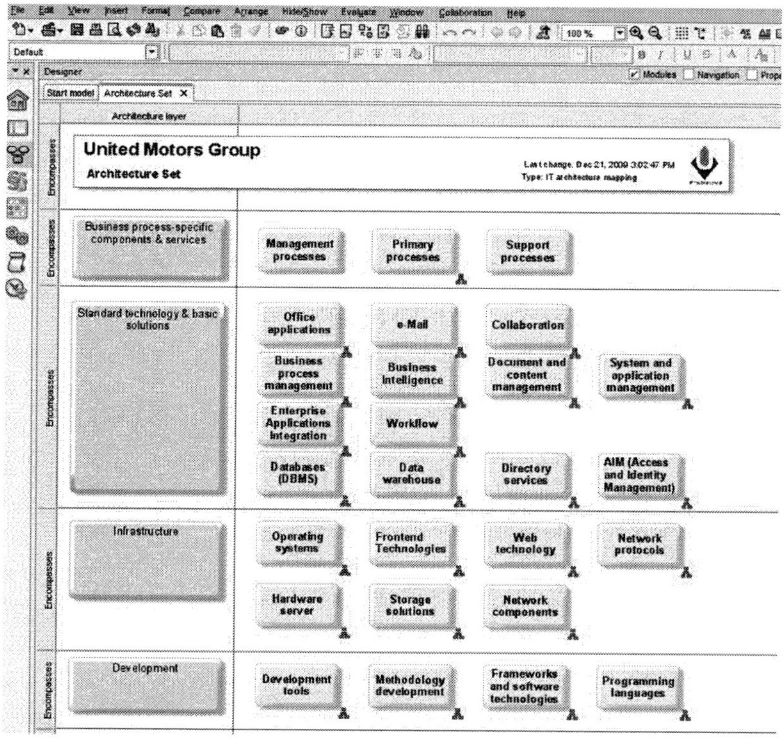

Figure 3-8: Architecture Set

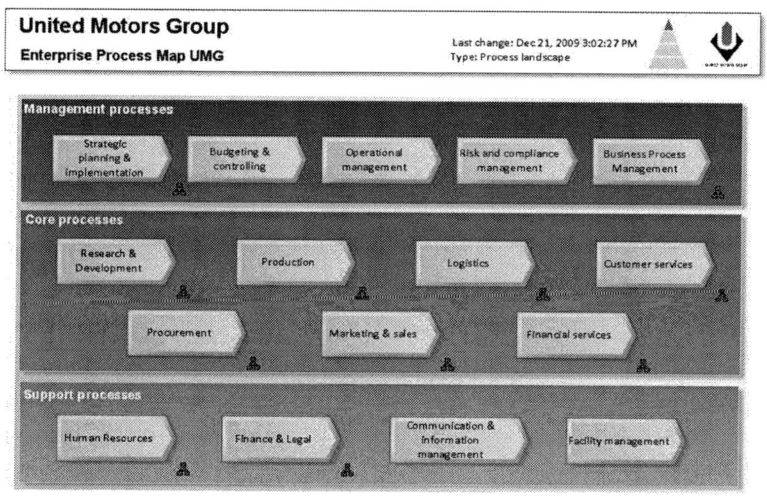

Figure 3-9: Business Process Architecture

- **IT Transformation**
  In IT Architecture Management, much effort is spent analyzing the as-is architecture, designing references and establishing principles. Based on these consolidated findings, you can create scenarios, roadmaps and to-be architectures [See Figure 3-10 and 3-11]. All this effort would be useless if you didn't actively drive the transformation from the as-is to the to-be architecture. IT transformation is about transforming your plans into reality. This IT transformation process can be technology-driven but it always must be in sync with business transformation efforts.

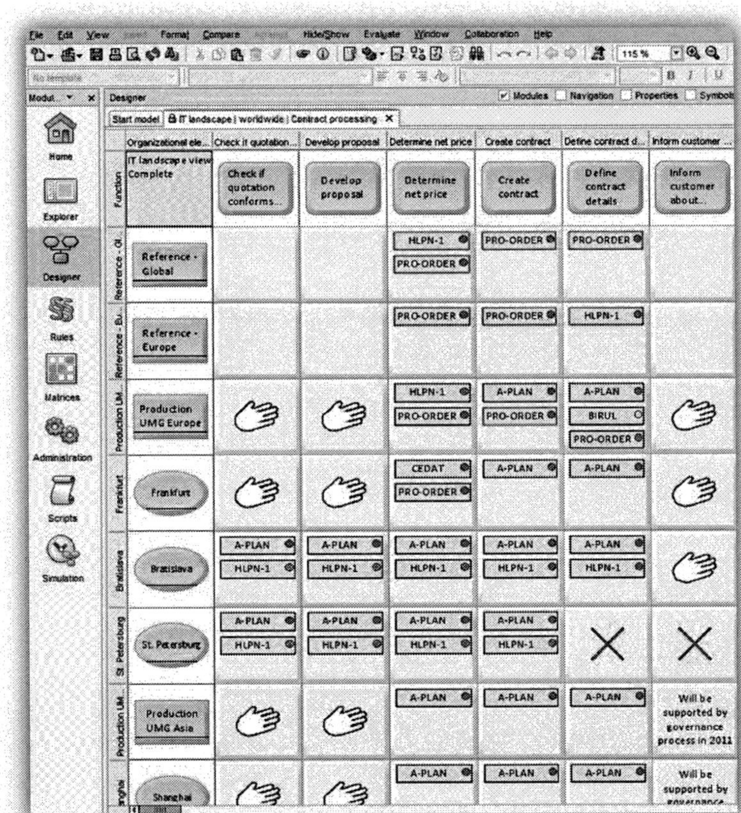

Figure 3-10: Process support map

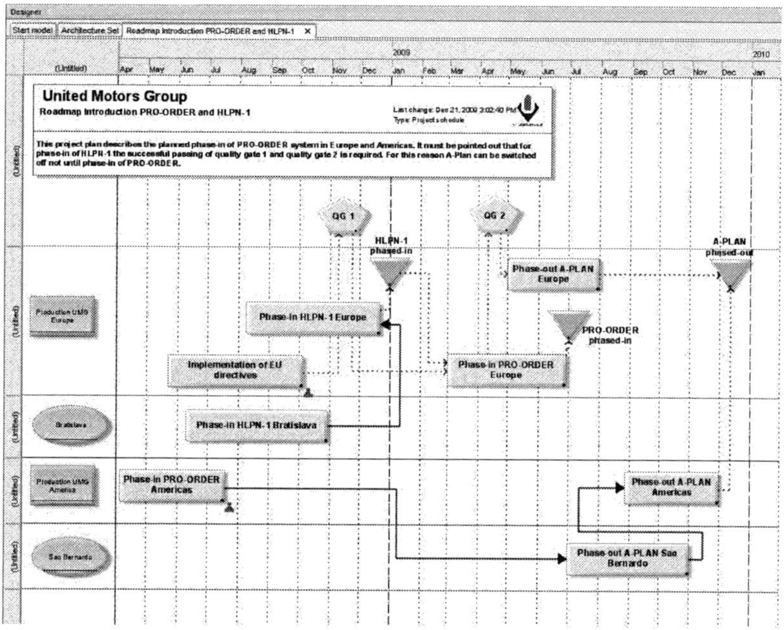

Figure 3-11: Application migration roadmap

- **Application Portfolio Management**
  Application Portfolio Management is used to justify and measure the business value of each application in comparison to the cost of maintenance and operations. The bottom line is that a "keep the lights on" strategy eats up IT budgets and eliminates the ability to support business innovation and growth while new applications intensify the biggest problem—a growing, uncontrolled application portfolio. Facing these major challenges, you need to actively drive the transformation of the application portfolio to support business growth rather than support just the rampant growth of the application landscape. [See Figure 3-12 and 3-13]

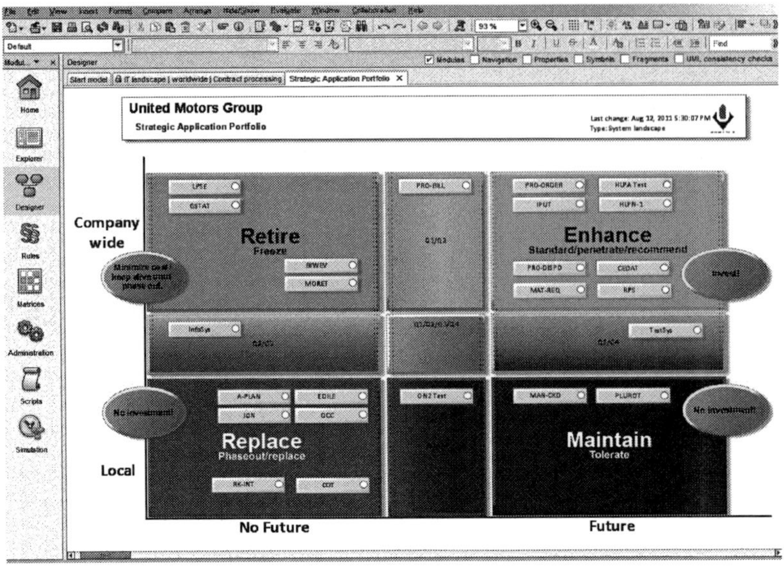

Figure 3-12: Strategic application portfolio

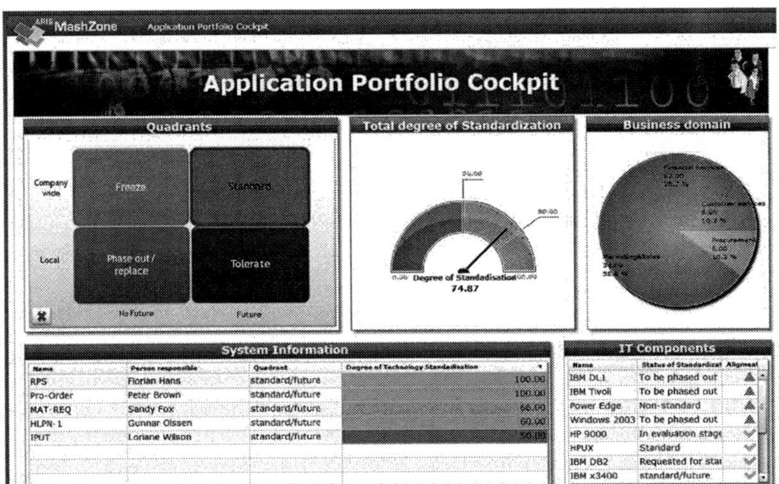

Figure 3-13: Application portfolio dashboard

- **IT Governance, Risk & Compliance (GRC)**
  Many companies are struggling to meet external stakeholders' expectations and keep up with the changing conditions of a complex regulatory environment. EA can be used as an enabler for GRC and is inevitable for all companies challenged to balance between managing risks and meeting regulatory requirements

while making better decisions and improving their overall efficiency. A combined approach of EA and GRC will enable your company to gain deeper insight into information security risks and threats, assess the impact of technology-related risks on business operations, leverage an integrated IT portfolio management and continuously improve risk management.

- **SOA Portfolio Management**
  Implementing an SOA Portfolio Management approach helps IT executives to transform IT assets and IT cost into business services that can be directly linked to business value and priced accordingly. As a result of this pure cost center, IT will change step by step into a service provider that adds value to the business with a transparent view into its operations. SOA Portfolio Management translates the EA vision into a reality of deployable services and ensures business capabilities are built according to business priorities. Companies can make better investment decisions based on the KPIs of the SOA deployment.

- **Frameworks and reference models**
  Using a tool that includes a variety of supported frameworks makes it easy to jump-start the development and implementation of an EA. ARIS reference models contain the knowledge of numerous companies captured by standardization bodies in industry-specific best practices [see Figure 3-14]:

  - **EA frameworks and methodologies:** TOGAF, ArchiMate, DoDAF, MODAF, NAF, SEAF, IAF, Zachman, TEAF, FEAF
  - **Templates for industrialization of IT:** ITIL, COBIT and COSO
  - **Industry models:** ARIS Telecom Reference Model (providing eTOM, SID and TAM), SCOR (created by the Supply Chain Council with ARIS and distributed freely to all SCC members), PCF - ARIS PCF (Process Classification Framework by APQC)

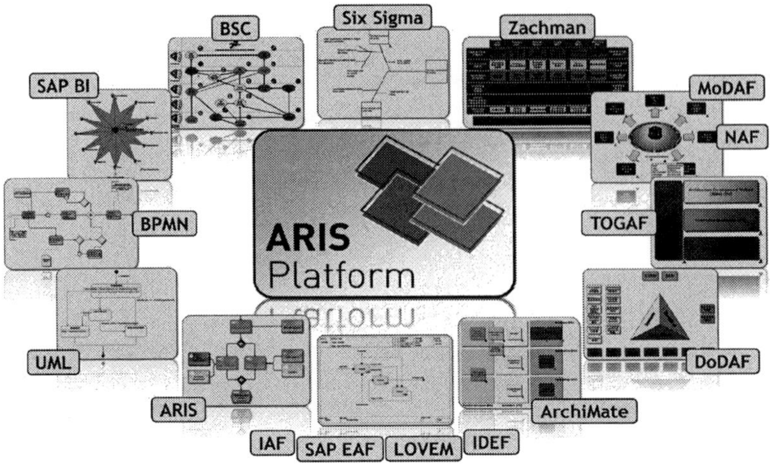

Figure 3-14: Frameworks and reference models provided in the ARIS Platform

How to Succeed With EA Management

Risk is a natural part of all projects. Maximize the success of your EA initiative by avoiding these five common mistakes:

1. **EA management is not a cure-all!**
   It is wishful thinking to believe EA is the answer to all of your company's challenges. Most EA projects run out of scope and fail due to lack of a clear goal definition. Objectives aren't well tested. First results can be achieved in short- and mid-term while losing sight of the big picture.

2. **EA management project teams—paper tigers?**
   More often than not, EA seems like a passing trend. If the buy-in from the management is missing, it's hard for the project owner to exploit the potential value of the EA initiative and to get support from the different stakeholders.

3. **Taking a random approach to EA management processes**
If you don't establish EA governance the right way, your EA will collapse because a clearly understandable and standardized definition of the EA processes is missing. As a consequence, the stakeholders won't act as a team. They will be confused how EA works in practice or in which logical order EA activities should take place and by whom they need to be executed.

4. **EA description—lost in translation**
Very often, the lack of a shared, meaningful enterprise-wide description method and poor integration of different EA perspectives prevent organizations from creating a holistic picture of what's going on in their businesses. As a consequence, the EA project is not firmly entrenched and cannot live up to its promise.

5. **Too many tools spoil the EA**
Organizations tend to use a diversity of tools and systems to manage their IT systems, document their business processes and standardize their technologies. Some of them may be standard applications. Others are customized or developed in-house. With such a diverse range of tools and data records, EA is doomed to failure.

Tips and Tricks

What makes the difference between success and failure of an EA project? There is neither a magical recipe nor a secret weapon. But using these six tips and tricks will help you keep sight of the big picture, achieve the benefits of an EA faster and also avoid common pitfalls.

1. **Don't do EA just for the sake of it**
   EA is a way to reach a goal and must deliver measurable and quantifiable benefits, such as the reduction of IT costs or the fulfillment of compliance issues. If you don't know your goal or how EA can help you to reach it, you will walk into a trap. Start with the result and assure that your stakeholders have a clear objective. Otherwise, your EA initiative will fail. Never forget what you actually want to achieve!

2. **Focus on people, not IT**
   Value employee engagement in the project. An EA is designed, developed and experienced by individuals, and the people on the project are much more important to its success than the tools they use. They work hard to deliver an excellent project. Don't waste your breath in pointless discussions. Choose a feasible strategy for working together effectively. Instead of focusing only on figures, place the emphasis on the emotional factor: Put people first.

3. **Start with the easy part**
   Great things start with small beginnings. Focus on quick time-to-value, demonstrate success and establish credibility. The best way to achieve this is by delivering some highly visible successes that can be understood by every stakeholder in the organization. Start with EA projects that are less expensive and can be completed quickly. Choose the EA use case that has high visibility and value across the organization.

4. **Make EA sexy, and spread the news like wildfire**
   Stakeholders are more likely to work with you if you persuade them that your efforts will make their jobs easier. To get sufficient support from all stakeholders and decision-makers, you must understand the challenges and objectives they have. Never forget about the power of communication. Invest time in educating the business people in your company about your EA program. Inform them about the value EA adds and prove you're not wasting their time to get the maximum possible guidance.

5. **Keep your EA healthy**
   EA governance is the basis for effective EA management since it monitors the health of your EA. Without effective EA governance, you won't be able to achieve architectural compliance or gain the confidence that all compliance issues are fulfilled. EA governance enables you to assess the impact of technology-related risks on business operations and reduce risks while also increasing the number of internal controls.

6. **Keep it short and simple**
   Have you developed an EA that looks like a plan for a rocket landing on the moon? Does it look like something people can actually accomplish? Go back and keep it simple. This will increase the chance that your stakeholders will understand and use it and that you will be able to maintain it. EA documents don't have to be excessive or impressive—they just need to be usable and understandable for your project team.

EA requires effort and investments in people, resources, money and time. Do it right to help assure the success of your Enterprise BPM program.

Where Do You Go From Here?

Is EA optional or mandatory? Well, at some point, you have to manage your IT organization. So the question is really: How should you do it? On a small or big scale? Should you take a business focus or use a purely technical focus? Are you satisfied with an antiquated approach that's focused only on technology, resulting in a limited view on computer systems and servers? Or, would you prefer a comprehensive, all-embracing approach that spans business and IT and touches every aspect of your organization?

In a world of constant business change, the future of technology will be about agility and flexibility. High-performance organizations require increased efficiency. They must create value with existing assets and invest in new technology innovations that guarantee and support sustainable growth.

Make sure your organization is equipped to keep up with change and react faster than ever.

Having EA management as an integrated part of your Enterprise BPM program will help improve productivity and performance by driving process excellence. Your management will be able to make better decisions about your assets based on a comprehensive view of the organization—a view that spans your IT landscape as well as your business strategy and the market in which your business competes.

The alignment is not the destination—it is a journey toward a joint understanding between business and IT. If you want your organization to be more than the sum of its parts, invest in EA.

EBPM Success – Linde Group

THE LINDE GROUP

Increased Efficiency

The Linde Group engineers an architecture that works for business & IT.

The Linde Group, a world-leading supplier of industrial, process and specialty gases and one of the most profitable engineering companies, wanted to improve IT performance. Working with ARIS and IDS Scheer Consulting, The Linde Group engineered a holistic enterprise architecture management solution. Now Linde has enormous insight into its application portfolio. Business and IT requirements and goals are in sync. Services are standardized, and the company has greater awareness of its IT capabilities, processes and responsibilities.

> *"Enterprise architecture management with ARIS has enabled us to consistently build on our IT systems. It provides transparency of everything from processes and applications to technology."*
>
> Thomas Steinich
> Head of Enterprise Services Application Architecture
> The Linde Group

For more examples of successes with Enterprise BPM, please go to www.softwareag.com/resources.

EBPM Success - Océ

Reduced process variants 30%

Océ reduces process variants by 30 percent. Now others will want to copy its example.

A complex IT infrastructure at Océ made it difficult to make fast decisions. So the printing company set out to become more flexible and agile—deploying ARIS products to harmonize processes and roles as well as standardize applications and infrastructure. ARIS provides "the single point of truth." It's where all information is stored on processes, organizational structures, applications, data and infrastructure. Harmonizing and standardizing business processes has reduced process variants by 30 percent. That's a result worth duplicating!

> *"ARIS allows us to work in a more customer-oriented way, which is one of the most important objectives... The number of duplicate processes has been drastically reduced, and ARIS is now a permanent component of our activities."*
>
> Jo Bleser
> VP, SPINE Program Director, Océ

For more examples of successes with Enterprise BPM, please go to www.softwareag.com/resources.

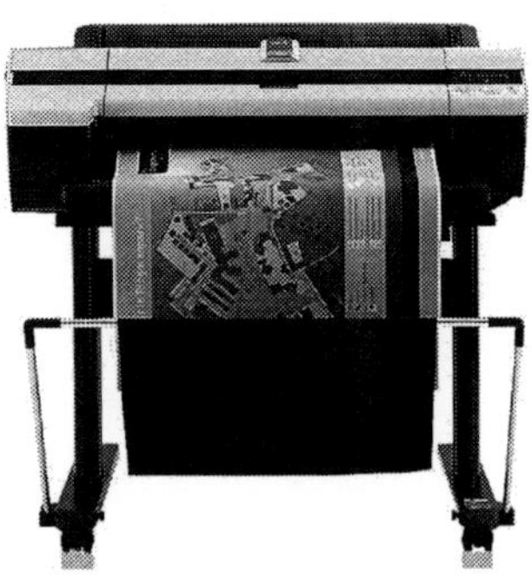

CHAPTER 4

BUSINESS PROCESS MANAGEMENT (BPM)—Automating Your Processes to Outperform Your Competition

INTRODUCTION

Get ready for insight into Business Process Management (BPM), another entry point into Enterprise BPM. This section goes into detail about the technical implementation and execution in an Enterprise BPM program.

Read on to learn how BPM opens up new ways to help your business do things faster—like open up a new sales channel or deliver customer orders. Discover how BPM enables your business to run smoother and consistently in an orchestrated way. With a true Enterprise BPM solution, you can implement and execute newly designed processes far easier than starting from scratch.

Of course, choosing the right approach to BPM makes all the difference to your success. So, in this white paper, you'll also learn about critical success factors, from stakeholders who play a key role in BPM projects to elements of BPM along with the importance of a proven methodology.

Let's get started in making you smarter about BPM.

WHY AUTOMATE YOUR PROCESSES?

In this section, we take a close look at BPM and the automation of processes. We will talk about different BPM patterns, stakeholders, elements and methodology.

But before we go on, a key question must be answered: Why should your organization automate your processes? The short answer is operational excellence, right-time monitoring and resulting cost reduction. Let's get more to the point and highlight four specific goals you can achieve through BPM.

GOAL 1: Consistency: it's better than rare moments of greatness.

Goal 1: Consistency

Moments of greatness are excellent. However, wouldn't it be nice if they didn't happen rarely but frequently? Carefully optimized business processes can help you achieve that. Good processes only add maximum value if they are followed in a consistent manner. Doing things consistently doesn't necessarily come natural to most people. You can't blame anyone for that. Sometimes people simply forget one thing or the other when they are performing a task or a series of tasks.

For example, you might know that a purchase order needs to be reviewed by three different colleagues but you simply forgot to put the third name in the "to" line of the email that you are manually sending out. Small, manual mistakes like that impact how fast your processes get completed and, in the worst case, they can lead to conflicts and bigger problems down the line.

Imagine how much smoother your processes would run if they were orchestrated automatically and consistently according to the way the process should run.

GOAL 2: Visibility into what has been done and what still needs to be done (and by whom).

Goal 2: Visibility

What happened to my sales order? What is the status of my purchase order? Who still needs to approve my pricing request? How are we doing on our business critical KPIs and are there any trends or patterns that we need to understand?

If you listen closely, you can hear all these questions being asked over and over in organizations everywhere. Often, it takes significant time to find the answers because you need to ask around to find the right contact, and then that contact probably has to spend time digging up the answer for you.

Imagine how much time you'd save if the process was orchestrated automatically and you could look up all relevant status information by yourself. Imagine how you can maximize business opportunities by understanding trends and patterns.

GOAL 3: Doing things faster and changing things faster than your competition.

Goal 3: Speed and agility

Speed and agility are key ingredients to being successful in a competitive environment. What does this mean and how does BPM apply? Increasing your speed means serving your customers faster. Ask yourself:

- How fast can you manufacture a product that's ordered?
- How fast can you answer a customer who's getting in touch with you?
- How fast can you process an order?

Amazon, for example, is known for delivering a package fast after an order is placed. That's because automated processes run faster than processes that rely on a lot of tasks like manual data entry and manual data validation. Automated processes ALWAYS run faster.

Increasing your agility means accelerating the way you can make changes in your organization. Ask yourself:

- How fast can you open up a new sales channel, perhaps via an iPhone app?
- How fast can you offer a new service with the goal of increasing customer satisfaction?
- How fast can you adjust your order process after your organization has bought another company so that IT systems and products can be integrated into the process?

In cases like this, IT is presented with a mess that it is supposed to fix within a very aggressive timeframe. Without a flexible infrastructure that allows for this kind of agility, IT has no chance to be successful.

Imagine how much more successful your organization would be if you served customers faster and could adapt to any change faster than your competition.

GOAL 4: Leveraging technology to innovate and do things that were impossible before.

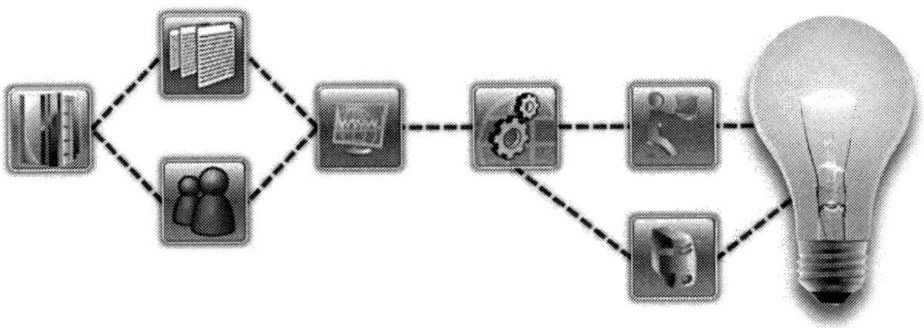

Goal 4: Leveraging technology

BPM enables your organization to realize opportunities that you previously didn't think were possible. Think for a minute what this might mean for you and your organization. Think along the lines of improving customer service, opening up new sales channels or offering new products.

Imagine having a process in place that allowed you to monitor customer behavior and react to it at exactly the right time to improve the customer experience.

THE BPM LANDSCAPE

To automate processes effectively, you need to know about the different usage patterns of BPM. The most common ones are often referred to as:

- System-centric
- Human-centric
- Document-centric

In reality, almost all business processes involve all three elements—systems, people and documents. But a process typically focuses on one or two main elements in particular. [See Figure 4-1]

Be sure that the Business Process Management System (BPMS) that you use for executing processes can accommodate all of these usage patterns. Your BPMS must be able to support the whole process landscape.

When your BPMS works with any of these patterns, you can move in any direction as your organization's process maturity evolves. You won't need to invest into another platform just because your organization has another usage pattern to support.

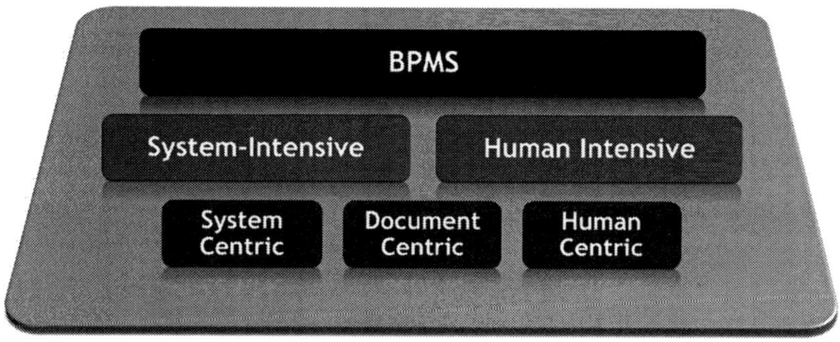

Figure 4-1: BPM Suites

System-Centric Processes

System- or integration-centric BPM is focused on integrating various systems or applications and orchestrating their usage based on the business logic as defined in a process. The execution of a process invokes capabilities of different back-end systems based on a sequence of steps that's necessary to complete the process.

A process may be completed without manual work (or human tasks), which is called straight-through processing. In most cases, however, processes include human tasks, which present the process worker with a user interface to review and complete necessary work.

A good example for such a process is an online credit application. The majority of the submitted applications get approved or rejected automatically without the need for a manual review. In such a case of integration-centric BPM, the majority of the process is performed by the process engine orchestrating different systems, such as ERP systems, databases, content management systems or domain-specific systems. So, it's essential to have solid and reliable monitoring and alerting in place.

The BPMS has to provide the ability to understand the status of the processes that are executed. If a process is stuck, the system must alert someone and should provide analytics and reporting to get to the bottom of the problem.

Such usage patterns require strong integration capabilities, the ability to work within a Service-Oriented Architecture (SOA) or to seamlessly tie into an existing SOA. Good monitoring and alerting capabilities along with effective problem resolution are essential.

Human-Centric Processes

Human- or people-centric BPM involves processes that require significant involvement by people for successful completion. Process participants might span departments and even organizations.

Two good examples of human-centric BPM are processes to establish and implement pricing for a product or to process an insurance claim. In such scenarios, the focus is on people working and collaborating together. The system has to provide everything necessary to make this human interaction and work as efficient as possible. The orchestration of human tasks, including delegation, escalation and collaboration, has to be facilitated by the BPMS. Process participants need to have role-based user interfaces and dashboards that help them to complete their tasks in the best possible way.

Document-Centric Processes

Document- or content-heavy processes are considered document- or content-centric. Most times, content like documents, forms and e-mail follow the path of the process. Over this process course, several people might version, enrich and review the content.

Starting, stopping or suspending a process based on an action, such as the creation, deletion or modification of content is also common in these processes. That means the BPMS has to integrate with one or more Enterprise Content Management (ECM) systems, archives or other sources in which content is stored and managed. It's worth noting that content-centric processes are often human-centric at the same time.

Let's look at an example of document-centric BPM: One of Europe's leading insurance groups receives approximately 7,500 pieces of mail each day. Each of these documents represents a workflow action in the organization. But sorting and forwarding these documents for action was taking too much time and effort. To tackle this problem, the insurer sought an automated BPM solution to automatically process and track the documents received each day, incorporating them into individual workflow processes.

Each document gets scanned using Optical Character Recognition (OCR) and then classified according to various criteria for further processing. The scanned documents start off an individual process for each next step.

Using business rules, the BPMS, in this case webMethods BPMS, manages the entire document flow up to the delivery in electronic workflow in-baskets. This process enables the organization's work on the newly arrived mail to begin that same day, rather than over a period of days.

By adopting this BPMS, the insurer shortened processing times from several days to one to two hours. The company also made it possible to more accurately assign documents to the responsible workers as well as to improve the tracking of each document.

For document-centric BPM, a BPMS needs to provide strong interoperability with any system that serves as content source. That requires the capability to search, retrieve, check in/check out and save modified content, for example. Interoperability should also cover the link between content actions (such as create, modify and delete) and process actions (such as start, stop and suspend).

Last but not least, the integration between the BPMS and the content source should provide a transparent relationship between content and process, so that it's possible to track which content was used in which process and vice versa. This ties in with process-driven Business Activity Monitoring (BAM) and provides a complete picture for auditing and compliance.

The Case for Adaptive Case Management (ACM)

Traditional BPMSs have their limitations in managing extremely dynamic and unstructured processes. That's why a new class of systems called Adaptive Case Management (ACM) or dynamic BPM is on the rise.

Focused on supporting knowledge workers rather than automation and efficiency, ACM includes a variety of functionality for problem-solving rather than transaction processing. For example:

Work is centered on a specific situation and a desired outcome for that case; the system supports the case worker with all tasks, rules, content artifacts and history related to the case resolution.

There may be little or no predefined process flow, with the worker defining the flow as the case progresses:

- The worker may add new tasks at any time during a case, either previously defined (including structured process snippets) or completely ad hoc
- Business rules may constrain the selection of specific tasks, or trigger other tasks and processes based on the user selection of tasks within a case
- External events may impact the course of a case either through automated processing of events or user reaction to the events

Human-focused and content-rich, the goal of ACM is to assist, not replace, human work. There are many business situations in which a person doesn't know the exact steps to take to complete an assignment. What is known is that the process needs to get started. Information that comes up during the process needs to be used to determine next steps.

Peter Drucker, the well-known management consultant, coined the term "management by objectives" to describe how these processes—and the people who participate in them—need to work: you set the goals, and let the person figure out the best way to do things in order to achieve that goal based on their skills and experience.

Case management systems combine aspects of BPMS, ECM, business rules and collaboration to effectively support knowledge workers, maintain a solid case history for auditing and also provide a reference for workers added part way through the case timeline. [See Figure 4-2]

Consider this example of case management: an insurance claims process. Claims processing is primarily a dynamic process in which the claims worker decides what tasks to perform and in what order. The claims worker may request information from the customer or other involved parties based on his assessment of the claim, then wait for that information to arrive in order to build up a complete, auditable claim file that supports his final decision. The goal of the process is to resolve the claim, not to perform specific tasks.

However, even this dynamic, unstructured case management scenario makes use of structured process fragments to complete some tasks: the original claim form and other supporting documents, if they arrive via paper or fax, will go through a structured data entry process before being seen by the claims worker as will other structured tasks, such as processing payments, once the claim is resolved.

However, the claims worker is unlikely to perform those structured tasks but works purely within the ACM environment. Proponents of ACM compare available offerings by using a specific definition of BPM that focuses on structured processes. This is a somewhat unfair comparison: they are actually comparing conventional BPMS tools based on older workflow and application integration approaches with a dynamic planning approach. There is nothing inherent in the definition of BPM—either as a management practice or the tools used to assist it—that prevents BPMS tools from including ACM functionality. Ultimately, both BPM and ACM are about managing business processes.

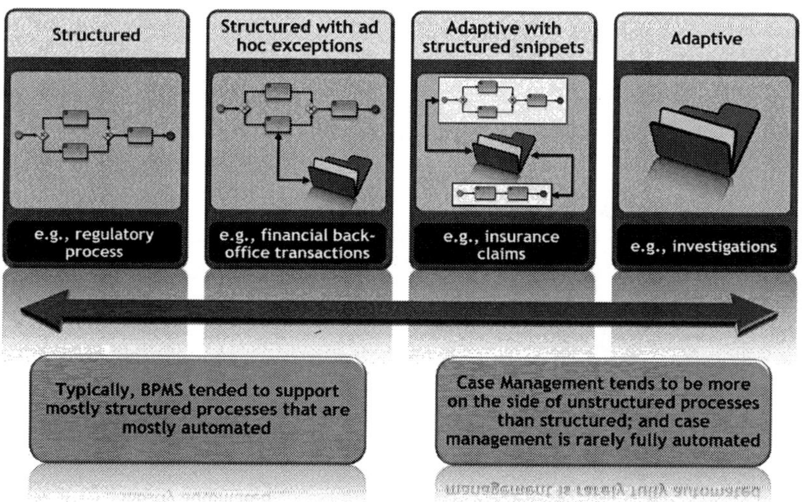

Figure 4-2: BPM and ACM managing business processes

THE ENTERPRISE BPM LIFECYCLE

As already covered, the six phases of the Enterprise BPM lifecycle take you through all the necessary steps to design, implement, automate and control your processes.

- Strategize - describe corporate strategy and map it to the business processes
- Design - define the enterprise processes, the resources that implement them and the business environment in which they operate
- Implement - transform business models into automated processes
- Compose - architect new processes and applications across the existing IT infrastructure
- Execute - deploy and manage processes across systems and people
- Monitor and Control - measure real time KPIs, analyze past history and resolve problems

Enterprise BPM lets you start at five different entry points—BPA, BPM, PI, EA management or GRC management. By combining them, you can achieve benefits quicker and ensure those results and approaches will be sustainable. For example, if you start with BPA where you design new and optimized process models, the subsequent implementation and execution of these processes will be a lot easier than having to start from scratch.

This section focuses on BPM, the entry point for (technical) process implementation, composition and execution.

BPM STAKEHOLDERS

Many people need to be involved in optimizing processes through BPM. Some of these roles were introduced in the section on BPA. We've expanded them here to include roles that are particularly important to BPM:

Chief Process Officer (CPO)

Defines Enterprise BPM strategy and objectives; establishes a process governance structure of process owners; owns the enterprise process map; ensures core processes deliver customer-driven performance; and meets strategic objectives.

Executive Process Sponsor

Leads and inspires development of core processes to deliver the very best for customers; defines the end-to-end process vision; assigns process ownership roles and communicates ownership and accountability; and champions process developments using process as a driver of business performance.

E2E Process Owner

Defines detailed End-to-End (E2E) process measures (KPIs); ensures the design of the E2E process; integrates and re-uses business unit processes; ensures customer satisfaction is measured and delivered and revenue and efficiency targets are met; ensures the E2E process aligns with corporate strategy; initiates and manages E2E process improvement initiatives; promotes standardization and optimization; and agrees on the impact to IT systems.

Process Architect

Defines the corporate process architecture; manages the enterprise process map and secures consensus and agreement; works with E2E process owners and process managers to ensure architectural conformance; and works with IT to promote business service re-use.

Process Manager

Manages day-to-day operation of business unit processes to targets set by E2E process owners; responsible for design of business unit processes, manages allocation of resources and ensures collection of agreed-upon KPIs; provides process infrastructure (such as documentation, systems and equipment) to support process users; and coordinates business unit process improvement.

Process Engineer

Undertakes detailed process design, analysis and improvement using agreed BPM standards, methods and tools; ensures processes meet process objectives and customer experience targets and are compliant with architectural standards; and verifies and validates that the processes are fit-for-purpose.

Process Developer

Drives the technical implementation of business processes, including defining human task applications, developing business rules and wiring process steps to services. As part of the technical implementation, the process developer is also responsible for simulation, test and deployment of the process.

Integration Developer

Is responsible for developing and provisioning technical services that support the business functions as defined by the process engineer. The process developer will leverage these services during the technical implementation of a business process.

Usability Expert (UX)

Designs the user interfaces that are part of an automated process and makes sure they are intuitive and easy to use. A process application's usability is critical in terms of user acceptance and adoption of the automated process. Usability and user experience should not be treated as an afterthought in a BPM initiative.

Web Developer

Creates the user interfaces that become the "face" of automated business processes and the touch-points with which process participants interact. The development of user interfaces includes the functionality that is presented to the user as well as the look and feel of the application. Web developers typically work hand-in-hand with usability experts.

MODEL-TO-EXECUTE (M2E): BPM BASED ON BPA

After the strategy and design phases of the Enterprise BPM lifecycle comes the implementation phase. The strategy phase has been used to define the business goals that have been consistently defined as single measurable KPIs. Following the design phase, in which the business units have documented their business process related requirements, is the challenge of implementing those processes within the existing IT framework.

Many questions are uncovered during the automation process, such as:

- How will business requirements be implemented?
- How will business and IT work in concert?
- How will work progress and be synchronized between business and IT?
- How will transparency be assured during implementation?

- How will a change request for already-implemented processes be handled?

For these challenges, use a Model-to-Execute (M2E) approach. Such an approach combines tool support and a procedural model and helps to achieve efficient, measurable and traceable results when transforming business processes into executable, (i.e. automated) processes.

M2E takes over all essential governance tasks, involves stakeholders at the right time and assures transparency during the entire transformation.

ALIGNING BUSINESS AND IT FOR BPM

Who is involved if we transform a business process into an automated and system supported process? How do all the participants interact? Where do we start the transformation process? What causes the BPM gap in the implementation phase? [See Figure 4-3]

All these questions are valuable. But first we need to understand which organizational units will be involved in the transformation. It's especially important to understand how the people in these units think and work while they describe their requirements or implement the process.

The Business Unit

The business unit defines its process requirements to achieve business goals. Often the requirement description is a high-level abstraction and doesn't cover all the details. Mostly these descriptions additionally cover unstructured information and leave much room for interpretation. Rarely will exceptions be documented within the process description.

The IT Unit

From the perspective of an IT unit, a process to be implemented needs to be described on a more detailed level. The technical implementation of a process doesn't leave much room for interpretation. Each and every exceptional situation must be covered and tackled. That's the only way to ensure that an automated process runs smoothly.

At the starting point of the implementation phase, the business hands over its process description to IT for implementation. IT begins to enrich the process description with the IT-related artifacts. Usually at this point the process content begins to diverge. There isn't a description that is accepted by both involved parties. On the one hand, there's the business-related description and, on the other hand, there's the more technical description. Both parties continuously work with their models, extend them based on their agenda, and hardly trace back the impact on the other side. Thus, the business process model does not reflect the technical reality any longer nor does the technical model reflect the business requirements. This causes the gap between business and IT to grow bigger and bigger.

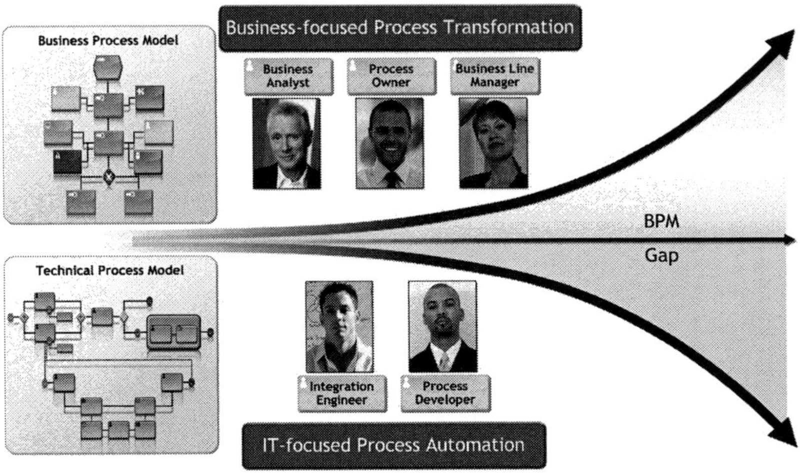

Figure 4-3: The BPM gap between business and IT

How a logical model gets IT & business working together

The solution for these challenges is often a logical model that improves the collaboration between business and IT. A logical model can be described in the Business Process Modeling Notation (BPMN). This description is a widely accepted standard in the business world. Business units and IT units both understand the notation. Furthermore, BPMN allows you to describe both business and technical requirements in a clear way that guarantees a smooth implementation.

The logical model is used as a communication interface between the business unit and the IT unit. All the relevant information from both sides can be reflected within a logical model.

Let's have a closer look at the procedures to implement a business process, using a logical model as the communication platform.

The business process, mostly described as an Event-driven Process Chain (EPC), will be automatically transformed into a BPMN model. This BPMN model provides the basis for an implementation and will be handed over to the IT department. From this logical model, a technical model will be derived for the real implementation.

The logical model will be kept as a neutral independent bridge between business and IT. It's also used as a synchronization interface between them.

Information that is not relevant to the business managers stays with the technical model. However, aspects of the technical description model can be synchronized back into the business model by using the logical model.

The scenario is comparable if we talk about changes made on the business side that need to be reflected into the IT world.

For example, let's say we have to implement a credit application process. From the business perspective, the process needs to be enriched by an additional step for risk management. As a consequence, this work step will be added to the business model, which is described as an EPC.

During an additional transformation of the business process (EPC) into the logical model (BPMN), a newly introduced work step gets introduced to the IT department. On this basis, IT can move forward to implement this new work step from a technical point of view.

All these activities are strictly governed. So after the business department has done its work, it passes the baton to the IT department. Changes in the technical model need to be assessed for their business relevancy and approved or rejected by the business modelers. As a result, models are synchronized considering the different views of business and IT. [See Figure 4-4]

Within an M2E scenario, the collaboration process between business and IT is technically supported and also partly automated. At each handover, the system automatically informs the affected department. Assigned tasks show exactly which department is responsible for the next step. So the interaction between business and IT is transparent at any point in time.

Between business and IT, the logical model remains the "constant factor" and synchronization point between both worlds. As changes are synchronized in both directions (from business to IT or vice versa), this is called a model round-trip.

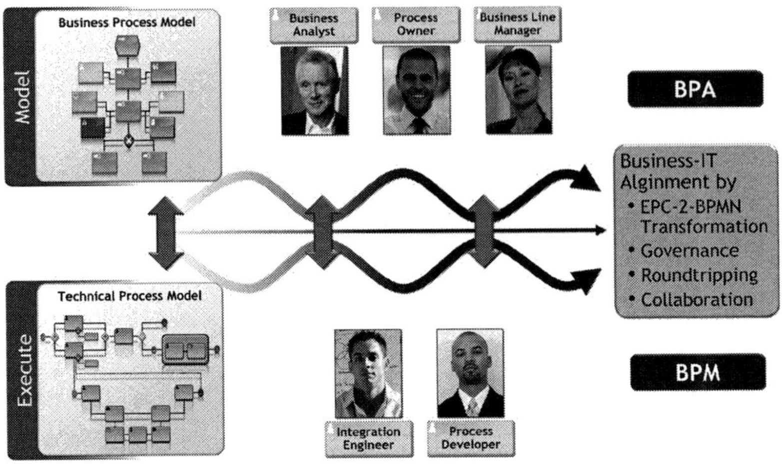

Figure 4-4: The technical model and the business model need to be synchronized regularly to avoid disconnects during implementation

ELEMENTS OF BPM

Let's go into the different elements of BPM. Understanding what they are and why they are important will help you succeed in your BPM initiative.

Process Models

Process models are used as the graphical description for business processes. Their structure reflects all work steps to be executed and their chronological order. Based on the level of detail, they contain information about data flow or information about the involved organizational units. Process models, on the one hand, are used for documentation, analysis and communications. On the other hand, they are the description base for a subsequent implementation within a workflow system.

Look at a process model from different perspectives, and you'll find content that is more or less relevant for the correlating viewpoint.

The focus of a business unit is mainly on the stringent description of the work steps relevant to ensure the company's business goals are met. Process models seen from the IT perspective are more detailed. They are mostly enriched with technical implementation details, such as used services or data elements.

Services

Services are used to exchange information between different applications. Standardization simplifies the information exchange between the applications' description and exchange format.

Services are offered via service providers and published via service directories. The description contains an exact definition of the offered callable methods, as well as a detailed description of all relevant input and output parameters. The user, also called a consumer, selects the suitable service based on its description and binds it to his application.

The communication itself is driven by messages, which will be exchanged via the services. A service will be called via its method interface. Parameters define the call and result in getting the requested information as return value.

To understand how a service call works, let's correlate it to a search engine. Searching for relevant information, you'd type the search expression in the input field of the search Web page. Depending on the implementation, the "search" method of a Web service will be called. Key words will be used as input parameter. As return value, the "search" method delivers the search result list where the content will be presented on Web pages.

Depending on the search results and the number of hits, the service delivers a long list of results. Often, the result is a simple confirmation that the service has been processed successfully.

If during an order process, customers' address data is written into a database, a Web service can be the right solution as well. The customers address data will be handed over to the Web service method "Save address data." The Web service then confirms the successful execution by returning a simple "OK."

Services are the most important elements used to automate a process when we talk about the exchange of information. In the same way the

Internet or e-mail are comfortable ways to exchange information across borders, so services will be used to exchange information within our application landscape.

Business Rules

Business rules can handle complex business decisions within business processes. As result, they deliver the information, where or in which way, to continue the process execution.

In the scope of a credit application process, a business rule can be used to decide based on various criteria if the request can be accepted or needs to be rejected. Various decisions, normally made by a bank employee during manual processing, can be automated and replaced by a single business rule.

Let's get a bit more concrete. Only if the credit requester has a constant income and the requested credit volume doesn't exceed a reference value will the business rule automatically approve the credit request. In any other cases, it will be rejected.

Very often business rules will be used in the context of plausibility checks. A business rule can control if the content of a user interface input mask is complete and consistent. Only when that's the case will the business rule allow continuation of the process. The definition what is meant by complete and consistent is part of the business rule logic and is described in the business rule.

The execution of business rules are handled by business rule engines. They are part of a BPMS or can be easily integrated.

Business rules offer these advantages:

- Complex decisions can be described comfortably using business rules. This save a lot effort compared to reflect these decisions step by step within the processes.
- The rule logic is strictly separate from the presentation-, data- or process-layer. Rule changes can be made completely independent from the application logic.

Nowadays, business rules are an indispensable standard in the automation of business processes. They contribute the process of automation and make subsequent changes something simple.

Business Events

Process flows are influenced by various events—for example, when a consumer cancels his order in an online shop, a shipped package gets lost or a package can't be delivered on time due to a traffic jam. All these events can influence the process flow. The earlier and more detailed information we get on the event, the better and more efficiently we can react.

Take a simple order process as an example. To get an order itself reflects such an event and is the trigger to start the order process. The article to be delivered will be packed, and the shipping papers will be prepared. Not until both events are notified that "articles are ready to ship" and "shipping papers ready" will the shipping actually start.

In the real world, millions of events occur daily and can be used to make our processes even more competitive, faster and efficient. These events are called complex events and the most effective BPM incorporates the complex relationships these events have with each other.

A payment process via credit card is a good example to understand the meaning of complex events. Let's say, for example, that a customer pays for some products by credit card in a small local shop. This type of event happens million times a day. Yet, let's say that just minutes later, another payment is made with the same credit card in a country far away. Let's assume that an unauthorized person is using the credit card data. The ability to recognize the relationship between such multi-dimensional events can be used to deactivate the credit card to protect against potential additional misuse until the circumstances have been clarified.

The realization and monitoring of such complex event relations is handled by Complex Event Processing (CEP) systems. They are able to identify event patterns, event trends or exceptions and they are able to react in the right manner if necessary.

Content

No process is complete without content. Content can be anything that goes along with our processes, such as documents, data fragments from an ERP system or information we present at the end of a process.

Content can have different states during a process instance. If we carry along a document in the process, it can initially be a draft, it can be under review or it can be released. That content is influenced by our processes.

In heterogeneous system landscapes, the challenge is getting access to the necessary content via an adequate interface. These interfaces are provided by a Content Service Platform (CSP). A CSP allows integration with almost all content repositories and makes their content available to be used in processes.

User Interfaces: The Face of BPM

A very important element to consider in BPM is the user interface, which enables interaction with the process. Efficient and ergonomic design is essential to a successful application. Even before an application delivers top performance, its usability via the user interface decides its success or failure.

Not to be underestimated, mobile devices are getting more and more important. They are well accepted and offer increasingly useful functionality.

Imagine a partially automated inventory process. Let's say an employee uses a tablet PC to scan the barcodes of all articles to be inventoried. He counts the number of pieces available per article and enters the number directly into the application's user interface. In the ongoing process, the information is synchronized with master data.

The historical approach to counting articles in inventory, documenting the result on paper and then manually synchronizing them with the master data seems ridiculous!

Why Process Intelligence Is Essential

Process Intelligence (PI) plays an important role in Enterprise BPM.

- With BPA, you set your expectations for processes by defining KPIs
- With BPM, you automate processes to operate faster
- With PI, you can measure and compare results against the pre-defined metrics

EBPM Success – AutoTrader.com

70,200 hours saved yearly

AutoTrader.com speeds up service using the webMethods BPM engine.

AutoTrader.com is the ultimate online solution for buying and selling cars and trucks. To maintain that status, the company must do all it can to rev up inventory levels and retain its thousands of dealerships/customers. The company standardizes on the webMethods Business Process Management Suite (BPMS) to bring new customer features to market—faster—and to improve internal collaboration. The first project delivered results in just 90 days. Using BPM, AutoTrader.com can report on daily inventory and show dealerships how to increase their ROI in AutoTrader.com products.

> *"Our customers can now see how to maximize the value of the money they spend on Internet advertising at AutoTrader.com and how to harness the great value proposition that we provide—increasing foot traffic at their dealerships."*
>
> Jai Siswawala
> Head of Integration and BPM Technologies, AutoTrader.com

For more examples of successes with Enterprise BPM, please go to www.softwareag.com/resources.

EBPM Success – Omnicom Media Group

OmnicomMediaGroup GERMANY

66% faster process

Omnicom Media Group's success is good advertising for Enterprise BPM.

Like any leader, Omnicom Media Group wanted to operate at top efficiency. So this leading media holding company used Enterprise Business Process Management from Software AG, starting with modeling processes in ARIS to automating them with webMethods BPMS. The project was completed faster than expected. After standardization, processes run 66 percent faster. That gives employees more time to improve client service. Value-added activities increased by 35 percent. System breakages are reduced by 75 percent.

> *"Working with Software AG and its product portfolio was the perfect supplement to the existing process work Omnicom Media Group Germany had already done with ARIS. The solution was built based on Omnicom Media Group Germany's previous experience in implementing an ARIS-based BPM governance system."*
>
> Roman Kornauka
> Director Business Operations, Omnicom Media Group

For more examples of successes with Enterprise BPM, please go to www.softwareag.com/resources.

CHAPTER 5

PROCESS INTELLIGENCE—
Improving Process Performance with Process Monitoring

INTRODUCTION

Management requires measurement. To manage a business process effectively, you must measure it—regularly, diligently and comprehensively. And, to manage business processes at the enterprise level, you must fully measure, analyze and respond to them across the whole of the enterprise.

This is the realm of Process Intelligence (PI)—having the tools and ability to see your business processes in action, and to see data and information in a process context.

This chapter tells you what you need to succeed with Process Intelligence (PI). In previous chapters, you learned about the complete Enterprise Business Process Management (EBPM) story and how you can use Business Process Analysis (BPA), BPM and Enterprise Architecture (EA) to implement your company strategy in your processes and to align your IT landscape with process goals.

In this chapter, you'll learn:

- What PI is and how it works
- How to keep processes running smoothly with effective measurement and characterization of business processes and process behaviors
- The role PI plays in the Enterprise BPM lifecycle
- The capabilities and features of PI and how to avoid pitfalls

So let's start increasing your knowledge of PI- because knowing is everything.

WHAT IS PI?

PI is having the ability to measure and control your business processes so you can make them more effective. With PI, you establish process controls to deliver improved product and service quality, productivity and profitability—first, by making process information more accessible and comprehensible, and then, by directly applying it to your business activities.

With PI, you can better leverage your investments in management methods, information systems and technology infrastructure to improve operational performance at every level.

> With Process Intelligence, you can:
>
> - Discover opportunities for improvement by seeing precisely where waste and loss are occurring
> - Know immediately when a business process, activity, or transaction encounters a delay or error
> - Uncover weaknesses and areas of exposure in any part of a process or activity
> - Understand the connections between high-level strategy and operational activities
> - See how value streams between you, your customers and your suppliers are working

In short, PI helps you adjust and tune your processes to compelling business advantage. Everyone involved in a process benefits–including executives, managers, process engineers, operations and technical staff.

PI enables proactive, fact-based optimization of activities and process behaviors. You can discover and resolve the root cause of problems instantly. You can respond to complex events in real-time. And by comparing current and past behaviors, you can even predict problems before they have an impact.

Because PI is so powerful, you can apply it to any business process such as order processing, service management, transaction banking and sales. PI applies to processes supporting almost any industry such as insurance, health care, energy and utilities, logistics and more.

THE WHYS AND HOWS OF PI

Successful process-oriented organizations translate strategy into action, define KPIs at every level and effectively manage the processes that drive business outcomes. These enterprises can synchronize their long-term strategic goals with the everyday tactical execution of their related processes. With PI, strategy can effectively be translated into the design, composition and execution of new and optimized processes. PI is a solution for the entire BPM lifecycle—at decision time and run-time and to analyze past history and monitor the execution of end-to-end processes in real-time.

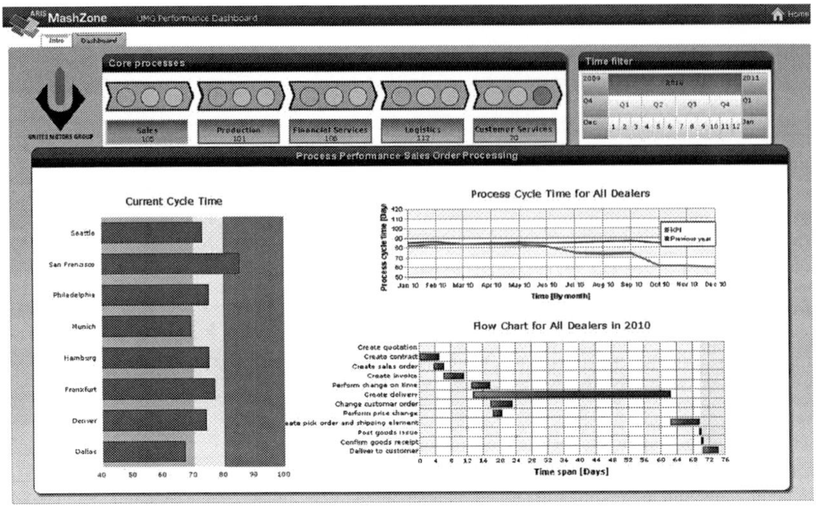

Analyze your business processes in terms of speed, cost, quality, quantity and other key measures, and turn your business into a higher-performing enterprise.

With PI, you can assess your business processes in terms of speed, cost, quality, quantity and other key measures, and turn your business into a higher-performing enterprise. You have the power to continuously adjust and improve the way your internal and external business processes perform. By understanding KPIs as they happen in live business processes, you can make objective decisions and realize your improvement potential.

Just imagine the impact you can have by easily identifying the factors that impact process effectiveness and by discovering and re-using best practices.

There's simply no other way to understand and manage your business to this degree of clarity and effectiveness.

What's In It for You

You aren't born with PI, and you don't just suddenly wake up one day with a towering process IQ. You develop your process knowledge and analytical capabilities over time. And what do you get as a result?

Better performance - Improved processes lead to better business performance; you're more competitive, make more money and serve your clients better.

An efficient early-warning system - Stop reacting after the fact by seeing critical KPIs (quantity, time, cost and quality) in real-time—and even predict potential outcomes.

Faster and better decisions - Identify process deficiencies more quickly, and take immediate corrective action before things get out of hand.

More with less - Get more out of your people, time and money by reducing waste and eliminating work errors.

Informative benchmarks - Understand what's happening now. Benchmark your processes so you know where to apply improvements and best practices.

Developing PI is the best and the fastest way to achieve these benefits. And you don't have to become a Six Sigma Black Belt or hire a bevy of programmers to make this happen! The capabilities of PI are now available to everyone. You'll read more about how to use these capabilities in the section "Capabilities of Process Intelligence".

Think Process—See Process

PI is partly in the ability to think about your business in process terms and partly in the ability to see those processes in action. You first must grow beyond thinking only about functions and start looking for outcomes. You have to really see your processes—in all their depth and detail, in aggregate and in pieces, individually and connected—to gain the insight and have the intelligence to know how they affect your business.

> When a process is **behaving**, you have the comfort of knowing everything is all right.
>
> When a process is **misbehaving**, you want to know *everything* about what's gone wrong.

PI gives you the ability to clearly see what's wrong from what's right. Once you set a limit, a threshold, a goal or a boundary condition for any KPI on any process, it's clear from that moment forward whether the process is misbehaving.

For this reason, most of your focus in PI is around understanding what's happening when things deviate or go wrong, so you can take corrective action in real-time.

Know Your Processes

Everyone needs constant up-to-date information about performance in his or her areas of responsibility. This includes the people who actively engaged in tactical and operational process, along with process owners and other stakeholders, especially customers and suppliers. With Process Intelligence, you have a running, real-time objective performance assessment of business fundamentals: speeds, costs, quality, quantities and risks—and the ability to identify areas for improvement.

> **See Your Processes Two Ways**
>
> - **Quantitative**, based on the measurement of objective end-to-end process indicators
> - **Qualitative**, based on graphical or organizational representations of the process structure

Operations staff needs to know what's going on within a process—as people are performing, as systems are running, as material is flowing, as energy is consumed and as transactions are processed. Sometimes, they need to know down to the tiniest level of detail—for a single instance, and at a single moment, such as a single order or individual part. They need immediate visibility, context and insight, and the intelligence to instantly make proper decisions.

Develop Your PI

PI is not someone you hire. It's not something performed by a consultant and delivered in a report. It's not something you outsource and have built for you, and it's not something you buy in a box. You develop your PI. It's built in three steps.

1. First, you need to understand the fundamentals of process behaviors.
2. Second, you select and configure the components of Process Intelligence.
3. Finally, you use the PI capabilities that deliver the information and control you need to achieve your target outcomes.

PI in the context of EBPM

The lifecycle of continuous improvement goes round and round. But change isn't supposed to be constant. Just like the rest of us, processes need stability, too. The successful result of a process improvement cycle is achieving a point of stability; you then stay on point to monitor and maintain control of the improved process. You must implement and tailor the intelligence capabilities, but you apply Process Intelligence most as you monitor and maintain control of stable processes.

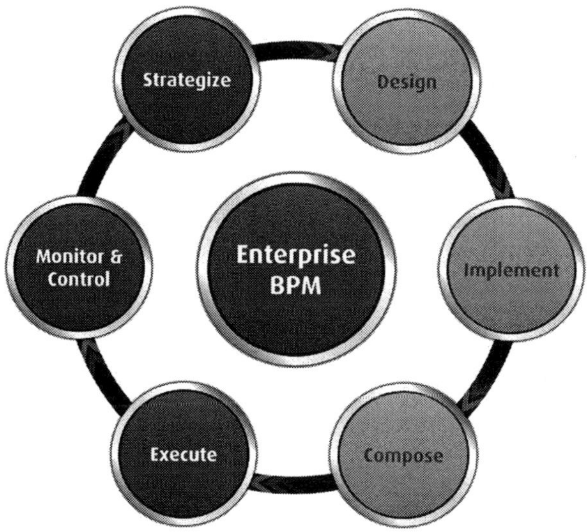

The Process Intelligence entry points in the Enterprise BPM Lifecycle

Once you can see your enterprise from a process perspective and have the intelligence to really know what's happening with your processes, you can boost performance in every corner of the enterprise.

You Don't Know What You Don't Know—Measure First!

It's always tempting to dismiss the current difficult conditions as the old way of working and to focus all your energy and attention on developing new and better ways. It can seem like a waste of time to spend any effort on what people may agree are broken processes. But don't run away so quickly. You must first understand the as-is state.

In the strategize phase of the lifecycle, you identify and select process areas for improvement. At this point, you must establish insight and understanding of the as-is processes, because if you don't, you won't know where the problems are and what to address in the design phase. Furthermore, you must effectively characterize your current conditions at the outset, so you will later know the value of the changes you've made when you've completed a cycle of improvement.

Experience also shows that teams tend to focus on identifying the main activities and the most desired paths, and omit the less common activities and paths. This is due in part to a lack of comprehensive modeling and a natural tendency to simplify the effort. But you need correctness and sufficient detail to support real-world analysis and the implementation of improvement. You want to capture all the sub-processes, paths and conditions.

> Insufficiently modeled processes miss critical process conditions. In the case of order processing and servicing, these could include:
>
> - When orders are unexpectedly modified by the customer
> - How orders are split apart by a supplier (due to delivery bottlenecks)
> - The way customers complain about invoices and service
> - When incoming payments are partial, or missing, and reminders are necessary

Because many various events occur in the real world, you need Process Intelligence to really understand what's happening. Knowledge about the actual structures and execution of each process instance is indispensable. You want to know things like:

- When and how often are orders modified?
- How often and in which scenarios are orders split?
- What were customers complaining about?
- How many reminders were necessary until the customer accepted and paid invoices in full?

Only with full knowledge of the as-is condition do you know to ask these questions and design this intelligence into your to-be state. Without this knowledge, you just don't know what you don't know.

Designing PI

As you design and compose new and improved processes, you must also define and configure the intelligence capabilities you'll need to effectively monitor and control them. Be sure to contemplate the new process designs and select the proper points of measurement, units of measure and the measurement timeframes or clock rates that enable process users and managers to monitor and control the new processes. These are likely to differ from the *measure-first* metrics you defined, collected and analyzed on the pre-optimized process.

1. Know where value is created or lost in the process. Expose the causes and indicators of cost increase or reduction, cost avoidance, operational effectiveness, revenue generation, and risk mitigation.
2. Measure characteristics such as volume, velocity, quality and/or special conditions. This may include identifying compound measures or figures of merit that represent KPIs.
3. Identify thresholds, limits and other boundary conditions that represent trigger-points, such that when conditions are violated, some form of notification or action must occur in order to keep the process in control.
4. Specify the actions to be taken when limits are exceeded. This may be as simple as sending someone a notification message or as complex as invoking alternative automated processes or procedures.

Remember that your PI solution must be designed, developed and implemented just like any other solution. In doing so, you must follow development lifecycle methodology that ensures proper architecture, definition, testing, documentation, training, and operational reliability and maintainability.

Measuring and Managing Improved Processes

Once you successfully move an improved process into the *execute* phase, you are operating this area of your business at a new level of performance. At this point, you must *monitor* and *control* the improved process. This is the full operational realm of PI: real-time management to optimize process performance and achieve desired outcomes. Deploy and apply the complete PI toolkit and utilize the capabilities to keep your processes in control and humming along.

- **Monitor process behavior in real-time.** Your PI solution will enable you to track the activities and events of processes as they occur in real-time. These can be tracked in aggregate or down to a single process instance, such as the tracking of an individual order. With the selected measurement characteristics, limits and actions properly configured, you can take specified actions based on process behavior. For example, if any order for over $10,000 is not processed within 12 hours, issue an alert to the active sales supervisor.

- **Analyze process performance information.** Use PI to collect and analyze information about processes. You may want to see a histogram distribution of process execution times on a daily basis and compare them to specification limits. You may then want to see a correlation of a key characteristic—such as geography or product line—to process execution times.
- **Process complex event data for patterns.** Unleash your PI solution on large and complex sets of event data and look for patterns that indicate key behaviors or trigger process exception actions.
- **Connect operational processes to strategy.** Apply PI to roll-up the aggregated behaviors and performance of operational processes and correlate them to business strategies or balance scorecards.

CAPABILITIES OF PI

Unless you're trained and experienced, process modeling can be somewhat of a mystery. It's easy to get off-track and model poorly—whether you're modeling the current as-is process or designing a new one. Process Intelligence capabilities help you overcome this challenge. They help discover existing processes and generate a graphical model of process instances. Furthermore, the results display precise details of this particular case and enable evaluation and analysis, also in real-time. [See Figure 5-1]

Today, it's indispensable to examine a business from the process perspective, in order to ensure your success and competitive advantage. Process Intelligence provides you all the capabilities you need to get the best performance out of your processes.

Use these capabilities during your Enterprise BPM program as soon as you want to:

- Visualize your KPIs
- React to events immediately
- Derive meaningful optimization measures
- Or even predict future events

Let's take a closer look at the different capabilities you can use to apply Process Intelligence at your company.

Dashboarding: Get the Optimal Overview of Your Indicators

PI provides a look at various indicators of your business. But how can you be sure that you see exactly the KPIs you're interested in?

Dashboarding enables you to monitor and analyze all relevant KPIs at a glance with situation-based and interactive dashboards. Deviations from planned values can be visualized immediately with traffic lights and speedometers. This allows you to discover if KPIs deviate from the planned value at first glance and to improve decision-making. The direct linkage of the KPIs to the process landscape allows a jump into underlying processes at any time to immediately examine the cause of the problem.

As you already know from Chapter Two of this book, you can define strategic KPIs during the strategy part of the EBPM lifecycle. With the help of dashboards, you have now the opportunity to see if they are really achieved. You can use the results to prove the success of a BPA, BPM, EA or a GRC project. If the values deviate from the defined target values, you can start with analyzing the corresponding KPI based on the results.

Imagine that your new company goal is to improve customer satisfaction. Your customers currently complain about long wait times for their orders. In your business strategy, you've defined that you must shorten the process cycle time of the order-to-cash process to improve customer satisfaction. So the next step is to have a closer look at the KPI "process cycle time." To do this, you decide to use a dashboard to analyze the actual KPI on a very high and aggregated level.

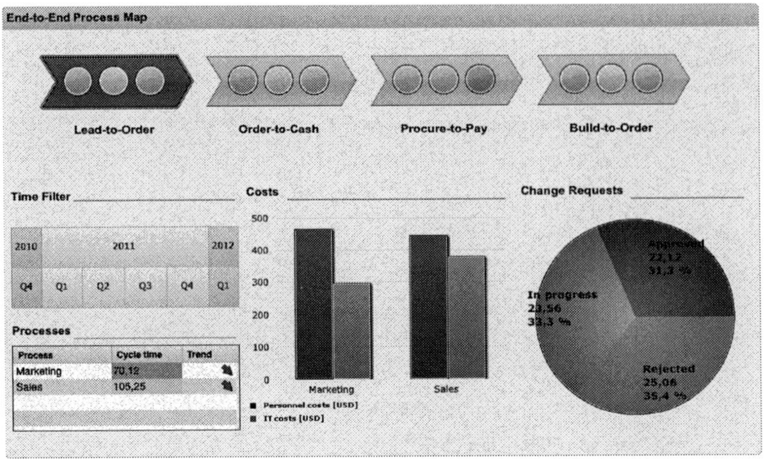

Figure 5-1: Real-time dashboard of the main process KPI's

With the help of the dashboard, you can see that the KPI doesn't fulfill the defined value. So you now know there is a problem. But what's the reason for it? Where is the problem exactly in the process? That means that the next step should be an opportunity to analyze the process that delivers the KPI to eliminate cause of deviation.

Process Discovery: Measure Automatically Rather Than Model Manually

To make decisions based on real KPIs, you should know the actual structure and execution of individual process instances. But do you know your process performance end-to-end and across all systems, such as Enterprise Resource Planning (ERP) or Customer Relationship Management (CRM) systems?

Process discovery *automatically* generates a graphical representation of your actual processes in your business workflows. To do this, process-relevant data and events are extracted automatically from the operational IT systems (e.g., ERP, CRM and middleware). This allows you to reconstruct an EPC visualization of each executed process instance from start to finish (such as customer order 123 from May 12 at 10:01 p.m.). [See Figure 5-2]

Unlike processes that are modeled manually, these process models are visualized not as they should be but as they actually are.

With process discovery, you have a graphical representation of the order-to-cash process. You can now monitor the performance of the complete process. You can measure and monitor the real executed process for further evaluations and analysis. But how can you use these results to identify and solve process bottlenecks?

Historical Process Mining: Identify Process Weaknesses

With process mining, process owners can analyze and optimize KPIs and discover relationships between KPIs, dimensions and process structures. Process mining capabilities enable you to generate an aggregated process view for each and every query dynamically, and analyze communication patterns and process behavior. Such interactive analysis lets you drill down into process behaviors as soon as KPIs (shown in the dashboard) deviate from planned values and identify the process bottlenecks that are affecting the KPI (such as lengthy processing times and high costs) directly in the automated measured process structure. You can select other dimensions at any time and get the results immediately.

For example, with process mining, you can analyze the automated measured order-to-cash process and drill down into the process to identify the bottleneck. One query could be: "What was the average cycle time of all 'order-to-cash' processes in the last month for sales organizations?" As a result, you will discover that the process cycle depends on the region in which the order was placed. Next, you'll want to know variations by region.

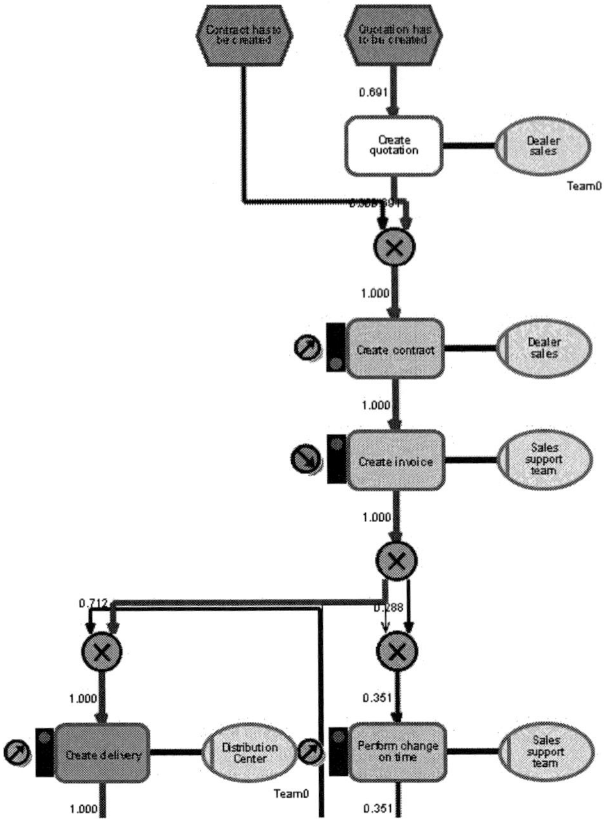

Figure 5-2: Automated, measured order-to-cash process. Trends and traffic lights highlight KPIs at certain parts of the process. Bold arrows graphically display the probability of passing through a certain path.

Benchmarking: Identify and Roll Out Best Practices

Benchmarking gives you the opportunity to compare different KPIs or process structures to identify the most effective processes. It also helps you discover the weaknesses and failure modes within the process. [See Figure 5-3]

So, for example, let's say that you know that the process cycle time varies across regions, so you can use process benchmarking to compare the different regions and identify the best and worst performers. You may find out that the lowest performer is in the Asia-Pacific region, for example. In comparison to the process structure of the other regions, you see there is an excessive number of order changes in the process in that region that are causing a long process cycle time. Now it's time to improve your process so Asia can perform as well as the other regions. Improve the process in Asia and visualize the success in the dashboard.

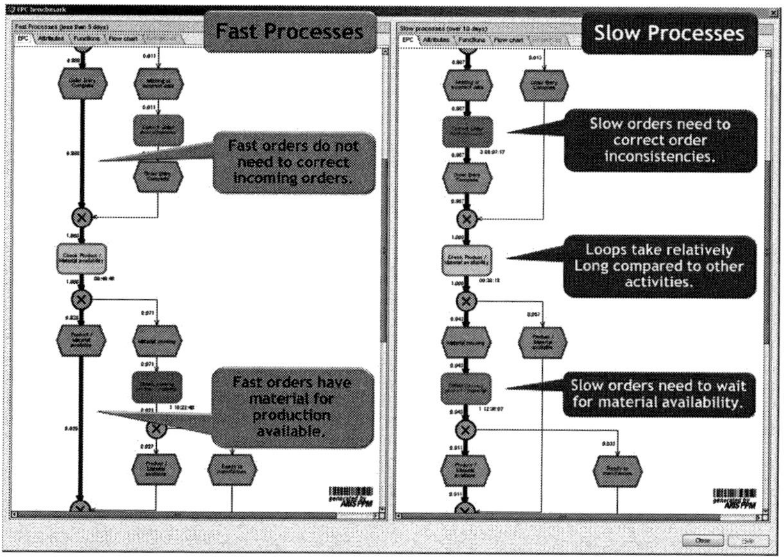

Figure 5-3: Using benchmarking to find process weaknesses

You now know that you can use PI to monitor and analyze historical KPIs with different analysis capabilities. You can use the results to identify and solve bottlenecks on a tactical base. But what if you could resolve problems immediately?

Financial transactions, logistics processes and customer relationship management are all examples of areas that require lightning-fast response times. After just one day, most of your data is already obsolete. To be competitive and react to events and circumstances in real-time, you have to be able to monitor operational processes regularly.

Business Activity Monitoring (BAM) and Alerting: Monitor in Real-Time

PI enables you to monitor your process KPIs and the flow of operational processes in real-time with Business Activity Monitoring (BAM). [See Figure 5-4]

With real-time insight into process activities, process owners receive actionable information and make informed decisions that quickly address problems. When potential problems occur, process owners can see which processes are deviating from the target conditions in real-time. They can also examine all involved process instances. Problems can be corrected before they affect your business and customers.

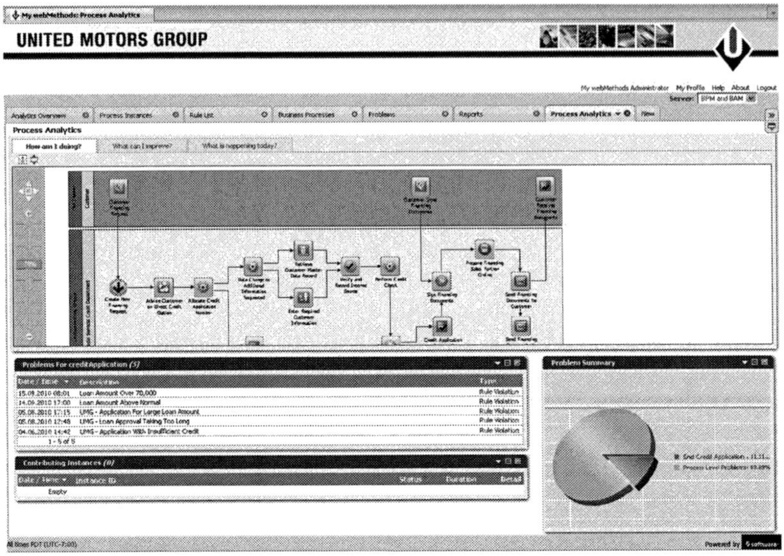

Figure 5-4: Business Activity Monitoring gives you real-time, actionable insight into process activity

This is accomplished through alerting capabilities that notify you when certain criteria are met or thresholds are exceeded. But these alerting values or KPIs are not necessarily pre-defined. PI systems also learn automatically how a "normal" KPI behaves, based on historical patterns, such as time-of-day or day-of-month, and can recognize if a KPI has left the "normal" range and alert the process owner automatically via email, SMS or Web services. The process owner can immediately open the corresponding process to identify and eliminate the current problems before operations—and customers—are impacted.

For example, BAM controls the supply chain by monitoring every order in real-time. As soon as an order varies from desired or historical behavior, the responsible persons are alerted automatically and can address the problem before it has an effect on the active business and customers.

Complex Event Processing (CEP)

If you are interested in analyzing extremely time-critical processes, data extraction and examination must keep pace. In this case, use the Complex Event Processing (CEP) capabilities of Process Intelligence.

CEP analyzes event streams to identify significant events faster than ever and triggers the right response at the right time. You monitor KPIs continuously and identify event patterns, trends and exceptions right away to identify and react to important events faster than ever.

In summary, the capabilities of PI help you to gain unprecedented understanding and control of your business. You can assess historical business processes—and identify optimization opportunities. You can measure business performance by monitoring and controlling operational processes. And you can see process performance at a glance, locate bottlenecks and fix them in real-time—before mistakes and variances impact customers or partners.

HOW TO SUCCEED WITH PI

So now you know the different capabilities of PI and how to use them. Be sure to advance your knowledge even further by exploring the most important pitfalls of Process Intelligence in Chapter One of the Intelligent Guide to Enterprise BPM.

In summary, here are the basic steps to success with PI:

Know what to measure

What you measure is what you are going to improve. In this case, you have to be sure that you measure the KPIs that are relevant for your business goals. You can have the best intentions in your improvement projects but, if the KPIs don't deliver the right input, you will derive the wrong measurements and fail.

Stay focused

Don't try to measure all KPIs. Reduce your KPIs to those that will provide insight into the processes that are most relevant for you. It is better to start with one process and then continue to the next after your first success.

PI is for everyone

You should involve all of the key business and IT stakeholders as early as possible so you can avoid conflicts. You need the business people to understand the business processes and to identify the correct KPIs. You also need the IT organization to support you to set up your Process Intelligence software and to extract the KPIs out of the different systems. Both sides should see *your* Process Intelligence project as *their* PI project.

EBPM Success – easyCredit

e@sy Credit®

Live in just 3 months

easyCredit teams up with webMethods for live business insights.

easyCredit added webMethods Business Events to its line-up to become a real-time event-driven enterprise. The bank gets continuous insights into its credit process and sees live incoming orders. This helps easyCredit comply with daily service level agreements. Live in just three months, the solution integrated easily with the bank's IT landscape. Intuitive dashboards display real-time event data across different systems. That speeds up decision-making and helps easyCredit score big with customers.

For more examples of successes with Enterprise BPM, please go to www.softwareag.com/resources.

EBPM Success – ABN Amro

ABN·AMRO

Live in just 3 months

webMethods BAM was "on the money" for ABN Amro's time-sensitive needs.

In the brokerage business, fast turnaround means everything. In fact, ABN Amro has service level agreements that guarantee it will process a customer's order in only a few seconds. Now ABN Amro has real-time insight into that process, thanks to a Software AG Business Activity Monitoring (BAM) solution—designed and implemented in only three months. The benefits are really adding up, since the bank has greater process control and can prevent performance problems.

For more examples of successes with Enterprise BPM, please go to www.softwareag.com/resources.

CHAPTER 6

GOVERNANCE, RISK AND COMPLIANCE MANAGEMENT (GRC)— Why Process-Driven GRC is the Only Way to Go

INTRODUCTION

Is Governance, Risk and Compliance (GRC) perceived as a burden to your company—one that slows down performance, costs a lot, eats up resources and doesn't provide any value? You can change that.

In the past, you may have kept compliant by documenting all your control activities and collecting the related evidence. But what happened when regulations increased? What if they overlapped? What if they changed? How did you know where your company was impacted? And, how did you know who to turn to get compliant again?

This GRC approach may have seemed like "easy street" at first. Over time, it became a rough road, quite challenging and slow-going. That's why process-driven GRC is the only way to go when you are implementing Enterprise BPM.

What if:

- Compliancy was a side effect of your enterprise risk management strategy?
- You could use GRC to increase your company's performance?
- Your next audit ran smoothly because external auditors already had all the information they needed?

With process-driven GRC, you'll align your company's business objectives with your risk management strategy—and be compliant at the same time. You'll save money because you can report at any time on how risks, regulations, controls and policies affect your company's performance.

SYNERGIES AND ADVANTAGES OF AN INTEGRATED GRC APPROACH

Most companies today have no link between their strategy, business objectives and performance management concerning mitigating risks and controls. Silos in business performance, risk management, compliance and audit make effective governance nearly impossible. The solution is to have a common goal: create synergies and advantages between performance management, risk management and compliance management.

Let's take a look at types of roles that typically participate in GRC:

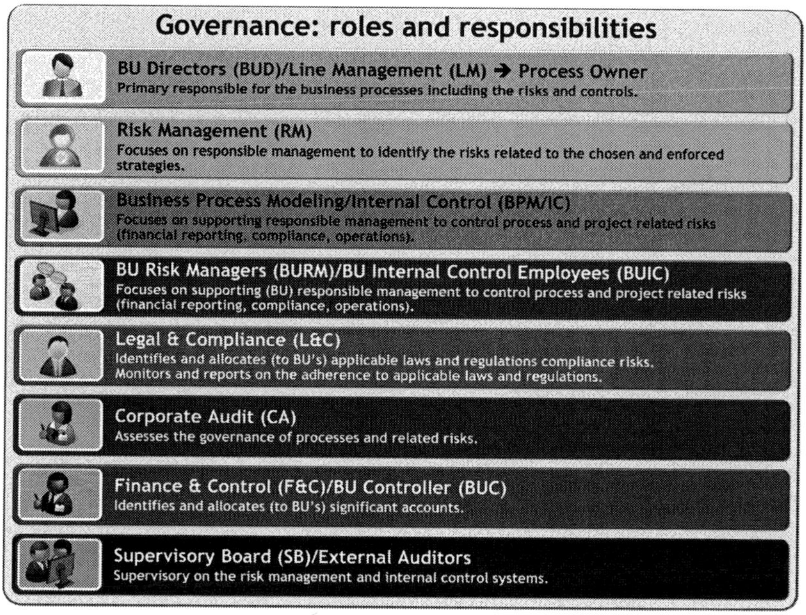

Typical roles involved in GRC activities

KEY ROLE OF BUSINESS PROCESS EXCELLENCE

How is your company's performance linked to risk management? To answer this, let's clarify what we mean by:

- Performance management
- Risk management
- Compliance management

Performance management identifies a company's critical success factors and goals. With performance management, you can measure and control your business processes to make them more effective. You can establish process control to improve quality, productivity and profitability—first, by making process information more accessible and then by applying process control to your business activities. Performance management monitors the outcome of executed processes and helps improve decision making.

Risk management focuses on identifying and evaluating risks regarding probability and financial impact. Risks can be derived from compelling events and measured by process and risk indicators from executed processes, just like with performance management.

Compliance management comprises three steps:

1. Defining your compliance scope (what laws, regulations and standards you need to comply with)
2. Analyzing and interpreting those regulations (translating them into specific control objectives in order to comply)
3. Embedding controls in your business processes

By following these three steps, it's easy to explain to external auditors:

- Which regulations impact the company
- How the regulation is interpreted
- What controls you use to implement the regulation

You can demonstrate your company's compliance by auditing and testing the controls regularly. By defining controls this way, you can cover multiple regulations at once with one control. This reduces auditing and testing activities tremendously.

With this integrated approach, controls in your business processes contribute to better performance and mitigate identified risks. Additionally, you can comply with several regulations simultaneously. This leads to Business Process Excellence and creates a single point of truth for stakeholders with different interests across the enterprise. This approach also completely supports the global standard of an Enterprise Risk Management (ERM) framework.

BALANCING RISK AND PERFORMANCE

Making the right decisions about business processes can be trying when there are conflicting interests. That's why you'll also need to find the optimal balance between risk and performance.

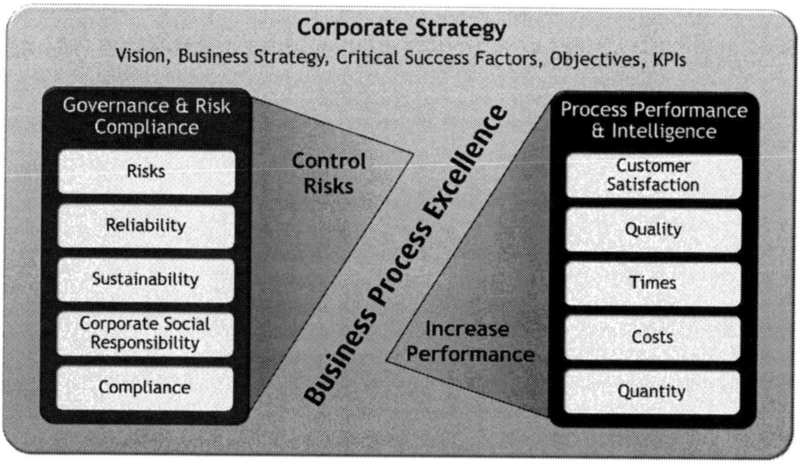

Figure 6-1: Balancing risks and performance to achieve Business Process Excellence

Imagine that your company focuses only on maximizing performance. It does everything to be the first and the fastest. If this sounds like your company, then you'll measure success according to performance KPIs related to turnover, profit, process cycle times, costs and customer satisfaction. See "Increase Performance" on the right of Figure 6-1. This approach works well—until you encounter too much risk.

At this point, you'll probably look at controlling risks as depicted on the left of Figure 6-1. But here's the catch: If you focus completely on avoiding risks then your company's performance will become incredibly slow. This is why you need to strike the right balance between managing performance and managing risks.

You can do this by using an integrated GRC management approach. You can design your key business processes to increase quality and speed, reduce cost and also mitigate risks. Considering your company's critical success factors (for example—why customers buy from you) will help you find the optimal balance between being performance-driven (concerned with speed, quality, agility, and taking chances) with being risk-aware (concerned with risk, loss and compliance).

The key is to make your business operations transparent and make decisions based on your corporate strategy and guidelines. Your management has to understand and analyze what happens in reality. This is why you need to connect a traditional performance management system (focused on financial indicators and regular reporting) with operational monitoring capabilities like PI and GRC analytics. Monitoring risk and business performance needs to be done simultaneously to enable timely decision making based on an enterprise-wide view.

HOW TO DEFINE YOUR ORGANIZATION AND ORGANIZATIONAL CULTURE

Integrate Your Governance, Risk Management & Compliance Departments

Most organizations operate in silos without an integrated GRC system that's aligned with corporate strategies and goals. This is a problem for your company's top management, which wants a GRC strategy that's in sync with corporate goals, and it also affects each and every risk manager in his or her daily work.

Risk managers deal with all kinds of risks: financial, strategic, operational, legal and compliance risks. To cover all these risks requires diverse domain knowledge and an integrated risk approach. The answer? Eliminate the different risk silos—integrate them and use one methodology for your business processes and your enterprise. By doing this, you'll gain enterprise-wide insights across risk areas, functions and connections between them.

Without an integrated approach to ERM, business managers have difficulty engaging front-line risk owners because risk information is hard to discover and maintain. Usually this information is in Microsoft® Excel® or Microsoft® Word® files. Content might be outdated. This makes it difficult to identify if your organization has covered the right risks adequately. What you need, instead, is a holistic view of all corporate risks aligned to business processes—not separate ad-hoc activities.

Risk managers will benefit from a holistic, integrated approach to GRC. So will process managers, compliance managers and audit managers.

Appoint an Executive-Level Chief Risk Officer

Since the head of risk management is often not a direct report of the CEO, risk management issues aren't on the CEO's radar. The problem magnifies when the GRC department heads report to different people who report to the CEO. In these cases, risk management lacks a single authority and the probability of unaddressed risks is very high. This is why your organization should appoint an executive-level Chief Risk Officer (CRO) who reports directly to the CEO.

Another option is to have the CRO report to the CFO, who is accountable for both well-implemented risk management and also BPM. Having both disciplines under one head makes it easier to monitor proper and on-time responses to issues and deficiencies in operational business processes.

Build a Risk Culture

This is an often-ignored concept even though a risk culture can "make or break" an organization. Without a risk culture, risk assessments and audit reports are swept under the carpet.

A risk mindset is developed when each employee understands risks and thinks through them while making daily business decisions. To make risk culture part of your organization's DNA, top management must "walk the talk." In addition, risk managers must continuously train and communicate with employees. ERM processes should be designed, approved and monitored by the process owners who are responsible for all risks in their own processes. The risk processes should be published on your company's process portal.

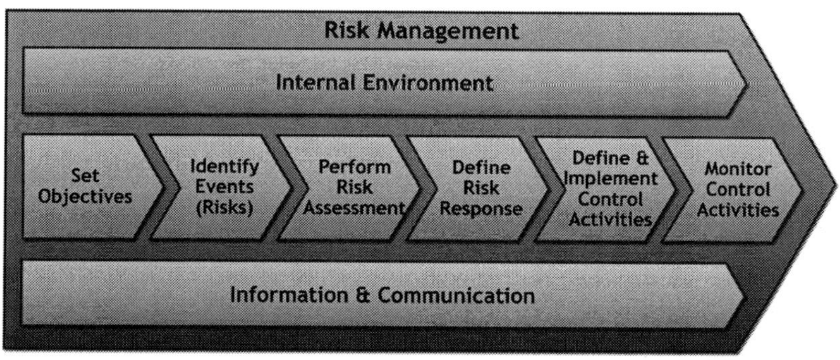

ERM activities captured in a process

Transparency is the key to building a viable risk culture in your company. Take a look at the reference process in Figure 6-2 as an example of a detailed ERM process with different roles assigned.

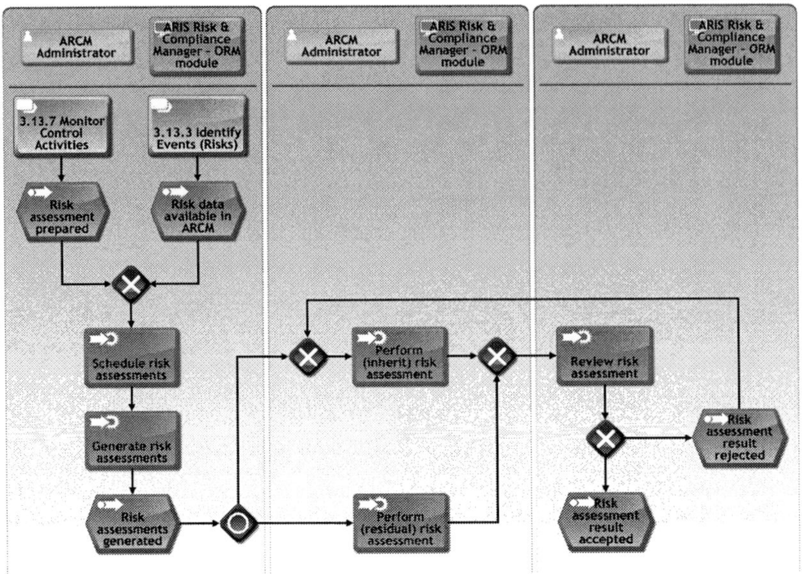

Figure 6-2: An ERM process with a detailed sub-process called "Perform Risk Assessment."

DEFINE A RISK STRATEGY

What is a Risk Management Strategy?

To identify events that prevent you from achieving your objectives, you need to start by clearly define the objectives. It's not enough to define a mission, a vision and strategic objectives. You also need to start by defining concrete and specific objectives. In doing this, consider the critical factors that impact your success or failure and how to measure these factors using KPIs.

As described in the chapter on BPA, you can use a balanced scorecard to define and visualize strategic objectives from various perspectives, such as from the customer perspective or a financial perspective.

With software such as ARIS, you can use diagrams to make concrete strategic objectives. You can define critical success factors and specific (sub) objectives and link them to the business processes that support achieving a specific objective.

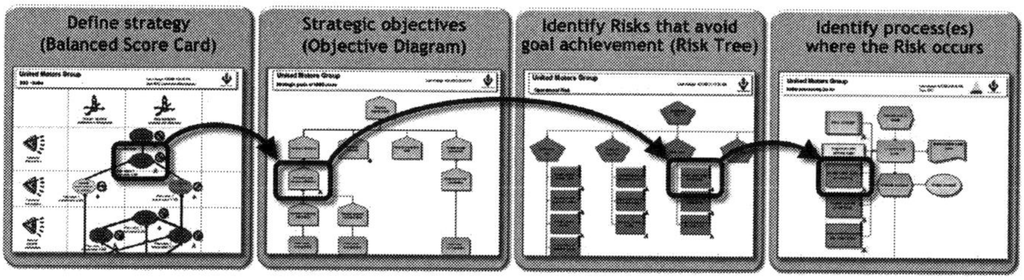

Direct correlation between strategy, risks and processes

Why is this important? Today, less than half of organizations have a formal risk strategy. In quite a few cases, risk departments conduct reviews, audits and analyses without a strategy. Because a clear direction is missing, risk managers are navigating "without a compass" when they attempt to manage organization risks just by using tactics.

Defining and Measuring Risk Tolerance

Risk tolerance can be described as the amount of risk business owners are willing to take to get the desired rewards. Only a few organizations have properly calculated their risk appetite. As a result, they sometimes take excessive risks when making business decisions. There is no scale against which to measure the risk!

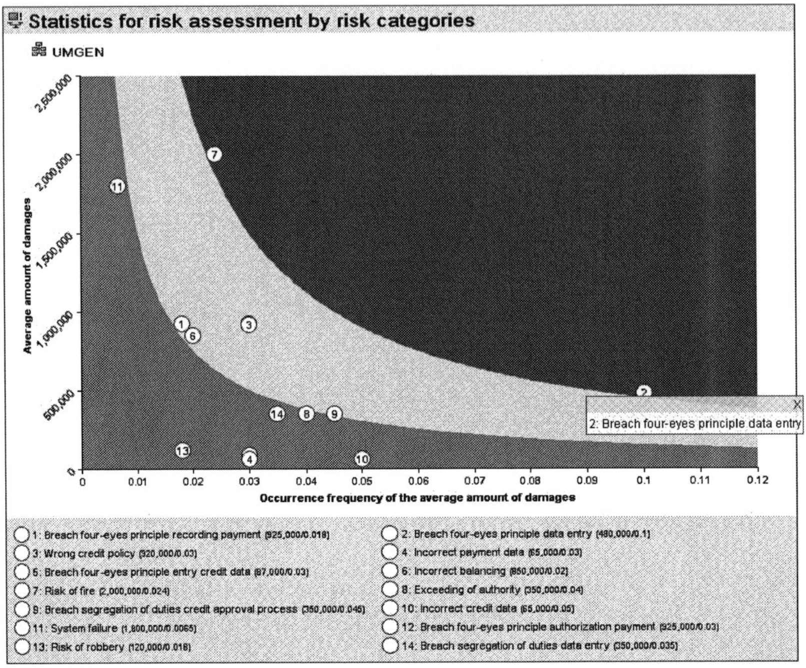

Figure 6-3: Risk thresholds help with decisions on how to respond to risks

On the other hand, organizations sometimes sit on a pile of cash and other assets. They don't take the required level of risks for business growth. By combining performance management and risk management, you can make good decisions to grow your business. But you should still keep in mind your company's defined risk tolerance. In Figure 6-3, you can see how the risk thresholds represent a company's defined risk appetite.

Identifying, Assessing and Analyzing Risks

Now that we've examined the organizational requirements for GRC and how to define a risk strategy, let's take a closer look at risk management. With risk management, you need to:

1. Identify your risks
2. Assess the identified risks
3. Analyze the risks

As a first step, look at your corporate objectives and related process context. Also define events that could influence your corporate objectives. Events with a positive impact can be defined as opportunities and channeled back to your managements' objective-setting process. Events with a potential negative outcome are defined as risks.

Cluster your risks into categories and KPI allocation diagrams to assure you have all the information you need about how these newly identified events affect your business and its processes. In these diagrams, you can define governance structures ownership and responsibility. You also can maintain risk attributes, such as risk description, risk type (strategic, operations, reporting or compliance), risk assessment instructions, affected laws and regulations.

With a process-driven GRC approach, you can easily connect yourself to other risk managers across the enterprise. The ability to assign tasks related to risk management and monitor the completion of these tasks makes it easy to engage anyone in the organizational process. As you assign tasks to a process manager, you can link these tasks to related business processes. All potential risks are shown automatically as the process manager accepts the tasks.

If you aren't sure you've covered all the risks, send out a questionnaire to the process stakeholders inquiring about potential risks. This makes it easy to engage anyone, including those with no risk management training, to share their expertise and also to warn them about risks.

As a next step, quantify the identified risks by their impact, likelihood and the effectiveness of their controls. For each of these dimensions, define a standard scoring measurement to be used across all business areas. You can assess the risk values qualitatively (in categories like low, medium and high) and quantitatively (in absolute percentages and monetary units).

Changes in score results can then be compared equally over time. Capturing the reasoning of participants simplifies re-evaluating assumptions over time, helping management to recognize when assumptions have changed and action is necessary. Residual and inherit scores are automatically calculated for each risk assessed, and they are used to summarize information at a strategic level.

It's important to define and agree on guidelines to make sure risk assessments are performed in a coherent way and the results are comparable across business areas. This is when it's helpful to use qualitative values (low, average and high) and corresponding qualitative evaluations (absolute percentages or monetary units).

Risk managers and executives can use this information to gain clean strategic insights. Results from risk managers can be aggregated and analyzed using reports in Microsoft® Excel® and PDF formats. Dashboards can illustrate all risk assessment results via heat maps.

A common language and a unified platform make identifying, assessing, mitigating and monitoring risks exponentially more efficient, visible and re-usable across other functional areas.

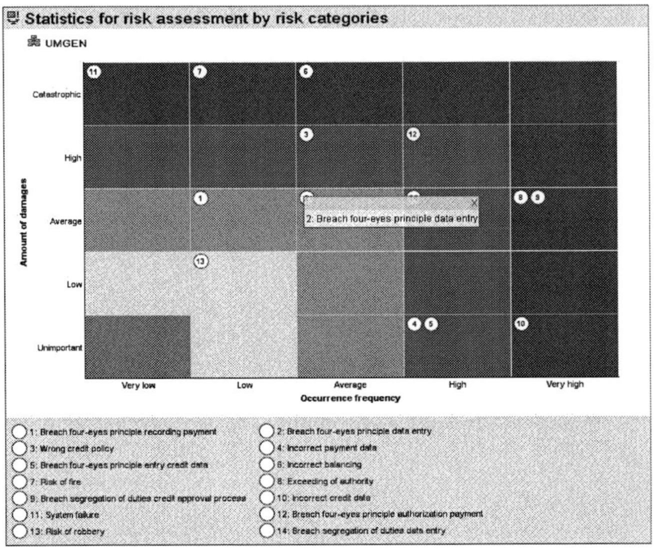

Figure 6-4: Risk assessment results presented in heat maps help in prioritizing resources

The heat map in Figure 6-4 uses shades of colors to depict occurred risks based on impact and likelihood. This view helps management prioritize resources for high-risk areas and reconsider the attention they give to less-critical areas.

Since all risk elements are linked to business processes, it's easy to identify where the same risk has been selected and assessed within the organization. If the same risk shows up in multiple areas, it's likely there are multiple controls in place with varying effectiveness for risk mitigation. This indicates where redundant controls and testing activities can be consolidated for stronger and more efficient entity-wide control.

The risk diagram makes it possible to uncover relationships between different areas. This closes the strategic gap between how top management thinks things run and how front-line managers say they actually run. Drilling down into any risk reveals the whole picture of that risk. Not only can you see the root-cause of the problem but also who is involved and what actions and steps are needed. This view can't be seen when there are silos.

HOW PROCESS-DRIVEN GRC BECOMES A BUSINESS ENABLER

Benefits of Using Risk Information to Decide on Risk Response

Once risks have been assessed, it's important to analyze the trend of risks over time using risk trend analysis. In the end, it's important to learn if investments in risk response are worth it. A prerequisite is that all risk assessment results, the mitigating control testing results and the process performance results are captured in one repository. This makes it much easier to decide on the appropriate risk response.

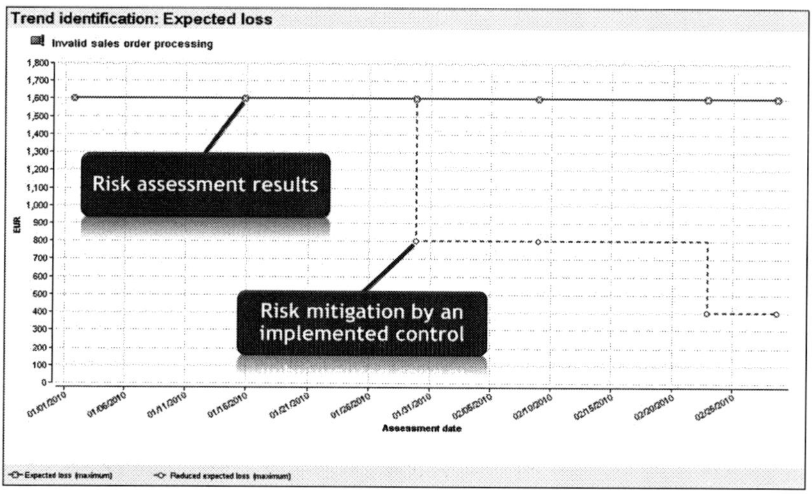

Risk trend analysis shows the impacts of investments of risk responses

Based on the risk assessment output, several responses are possible for the assessed risk. Risks can be avoided, accepted, reduced or shared. Often line management, supported by a business risk manager, decides on appropriate risk response. A response can also be a set of actions to align risks with the entity's risk tolerances and risk appetite.

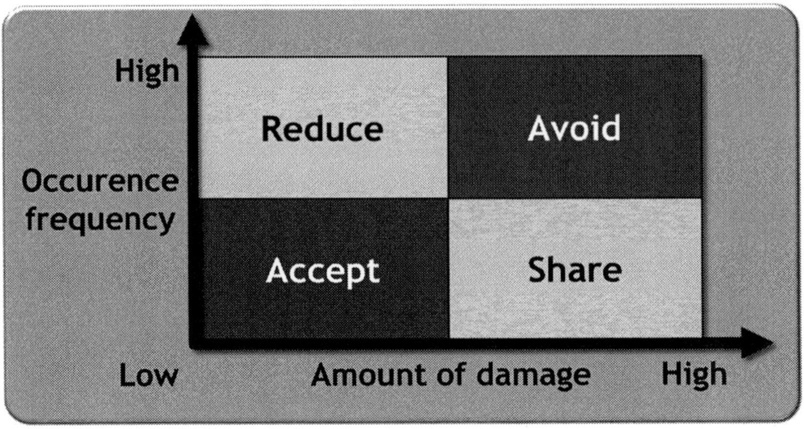

Risk response quadrant provides guidance

Four possible risk responses are:

1. Reduce risk—for example, by implementing a mitigating process control
2. Share risk—for example, by getting insurance
3. Accept risk—for example, the risk is tolerated because the costs of mitigation is not worth it
4. Avoid risk—for example, by shutting down a risk-prone location

After you've decided how to react to your risk, you need to take action by installing a control that either reduces shares or avoids that risk. Often, more than one control is needed to mitigate one risk. It's important to be sure that the costs to control the risk are in sync with the potential cost of the risk.

Controls are now defined and related to the risk that is mitigated by the control. Of course, you also need to define ownership for this control and implement it as part of the actual business process execution. Based on the criticality of the control, decisions are made regarding if, when and how the control should be tested.

One way of helping risk managers reduce existing work is by identifying low-risk impacted areas and uncovering controls that can be consolidated or leveraging existing work to avoid redundancies. The result is a one-third reduction of time the organization currently spends needed for assessing, mitigation and monitoring risk activities.

Benefits of Process Discovery

Even for critical, primary end-to-end processes, many companies are not completely sure about the actual process structure and execution of their processes instances sequence. If you don't know how the actual process is executed, you can't accurately identify the risks and the mitigating controls. Sometimes workarounds in the system or loops in the process are simply not recognized. It's better to measure automatically rather than model manually, and it's crucial that the process design is valid. An approach to do this simply and reliably is by using process discovery technology.

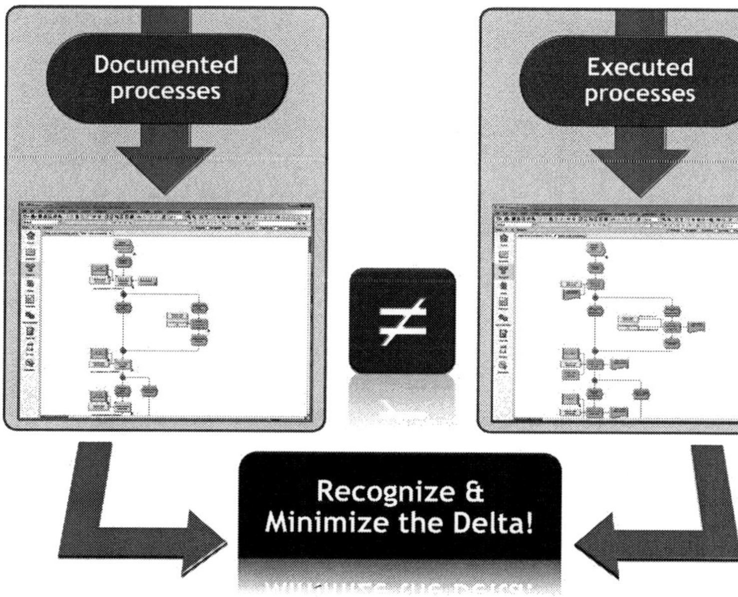

Process discovery identifies if the documented processes are being followed

The actual executed process is measured and documented in such a way that the identified risks and mitigating controls can be added later to the process design. Other advantages are that it's possible to do automated risk and bottleneck analyses, and you can combine process performance with risk and compliance performance for the same process.

The comparison of documented processes to executed processes gives risk managers insights as to where improvements should be made. If you need to improve business performance, look for redundant controls in the process chain that can be deleted to reduce process cycle time. If performance is not the issue but risks are, then make improvements by adding process controls for example. After implementing these changes, processes can be measured again to see the effects of the implemented changes.

Benefits of Reporting

As you know from the chapter on PI, you can synchronize your company's long-term strategic goals with the everyday tactical execution of their related processes. Of course, risk managers need to closely watch the results of their ERM program. By monitoring and analyzing all relevant KPIs and Key Risk Indicators (KRIs), you can continuously adjust and improve your ERM strategy and the performance of your business processes. If it impacts your company, you can be sure to find it. If a control, for example, is not effective, an issue can be initiated and monitored as well.

Graphical representations can be easily customized for individuals based on their roles and responsibilities. Risk managers can benefit from a common GRC approach and dashboarding. Transparency for end users, business managers, auditors and others can be achieved by using a process portal with risk and controls embedded in the process design, including business roles, application systems and segregation of duties.

Looking for more insight on GRC? Visit www.grc-lounge.com.

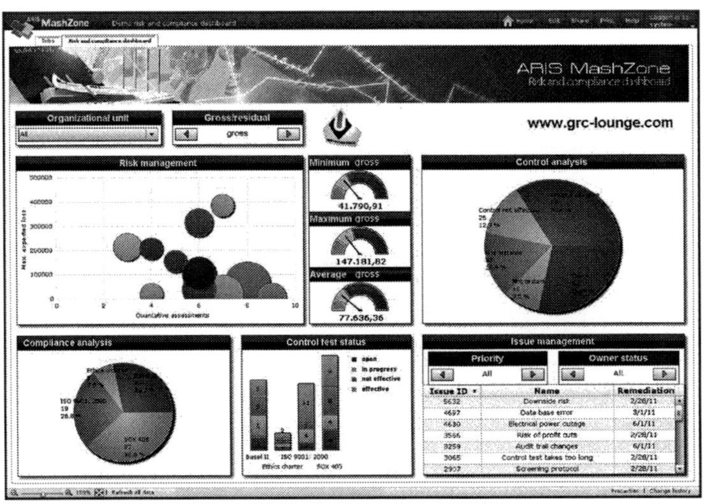

Risk & Compliance Dashboard shows the different status for assessed risks, installed controls, test of controls, created issues and provides an overview about the compliance status of your company.

EBPM Success - MN

Improved decision-making

MN finds that managing risks is no risk with Software AG.

MN has chosen a risk-focused approach to connect strategic objectives with risk assessments and process controls. Supported by the ARIS Platform and Software AG Consulting, MN developed and implemented a risk governance framework. Its integrated approach has increased risk awareness enterprise-wide, enabling the company to identify and manage risks better while simultaneously improving process quality and decision-making.

For more examples of successes with Enterprise BPM, please go to www.softwareag.com/resources.

EBPM Success – Hitachi

HITACHI

40% cost reduction

Hitachi Construction Machinery Europe digs up 40 percent cost savings by using ARIS.

Complying with regulations was a tough job for Hitachi Construction Machinery Europe. Audit-driven internal control resulted in a heavy workload and high consulting fees. Workload and costs are lighter now, thanks to ARIS. A highly automated, business-driven internal-control process assures compliance with various laws and regulations at 40 percent less internal cost. Other benefits Hitachi really digs include reduced reporting, better insight for improved decision-making and better governance to reduce risk.

For more examples of successes with Enterprise BPM, please go to www.softwareag.com/resources.

SUMMARY

More and more organizations realize that process improvement can never reach its full potential if it is stuck in isolated departments and accessible by a few selected stakeholders. To unleash process power it is essential to bring **people, processes and technology** together in a sustainable Enterprise BPM (EBPM) program.

Often the question is how to start with such a program. First, get the right **people** around you. You will have business people with an interest in IT and IT people with an interest in business. Then leverage your network to identify and engage these individuals.

Identify core **processes** where improvements could make a real difference. Set up a pilot and describe, optimize, automate and measure these processes. Don't forget to ensure C-Level sponsorship (see chapter 1), to reflect your corporate strategy (see chapter 2), to map your IT landscape (see chapter 3) to measure first (chapter 5) and to reflect risks and regulations (see chapter 6). Grow from one process to another to ensure fast results.

Build your EBPM program on the right **technology**. This technology should support and integrate all ongoing initiatives, like Business Process Analysis, Enterprise Architecture Management, Business Process Management, Process Intelligence and Governance Risk & Compliance Management. All initiatives should be technically integrated to ensure that you get a holistic end-to-end perspective of your enterprise. All stakeholders must be empowered through state of the art collaboration capabilities. The more collaboration you have, the more governance you need. Therefore, process governance should also be supported by your technology of choice. And of course your technology should be able to grow with the demands of your business.

When having completed your EBPM journey you will have reached a new level of business agility. But don't forget: EBPM is never-ending. The perfect process of today might be an outdated process tomorrow.

Therefore, we will continuously launch new chapters of this book to keep you informed of the evolution of Enterprise BPM. Please visit www.softwareag.com/ebpm for more information.

In the meantime, follow our blog to provide your feedback on the state of BPM in your organization, discuss new BPM trends, and share your best practices or pitfalls. Let's collaborate to help the worldwide BPM community shape the future of business agility: http://blog.softwareag.com.

RESOURCES

Websites:

www.softwareag.com/enterprisebpm

www.process-intelligence.com

www.itmodernization.com

www.bptrends.com

www.softwareag.com/ebpm

www.process-intelligence.com

www.itmodernization.com

www.bptrends.com

www.alexosterwalder.com

www.grc-lounge.com

Blogs:

Software AG's Blog: http://blog.softwareag.com

ARIS BPM Community: www.ariscommunity.com

Sandy Kemsley's BPM Blog: www.column2.com

ARIS BPM Community: www.ariscommunity.com

Sandy Kemsley's BPM Blog: www.column2.com

Books:

Don't miss our free "Dummies" book series

It's a great start into BPM, Service-Oriented Architecture (SOA), Process Intelligence and Master Data Management: http://www.softwareag.com/dummies

"*ARIS Design Platform: Getting Started with BPM*", Rob Davis & Eric Brabaender, Springer 2007

"*ARIS Design Platform: Advanced Process Modeling and Administration*", Rob Davis, Springer 2008